T0278335

Praise for *The Wounds Are the Witness*

"As Howard Thurman preaches in her right ear, as James Baldwin prophesies in her left, as Pauli Murray prays over her, and as Zora Neale Hurston prepares a path before her, Yolanda Pierce shapes a majestic theology of sound and crafts a masterly psychology of voice. *The Wounds Are the Witness* is where Teilhard de Chardin meets Beyoncé, as Pierce takes the world to church with sacred speech that transforms trauma, heals hurts, rejoices in justice, and celebrates spirit. In this brilliant book, we hear the testimony of arguably the greatest interpreter of religion for the thinking public in our present age."

—**Michael Eric Dyson**, professor, commentator,
and *New York Times*–bestselling author of
Tears We Cannot Stop and other books

"Yolanda Pierce provides a celebration of the diverse ways the Black church nurtures gifts of leadership and moral power, gifts that are so needed for the facing of twenty-first-century crises. Pierce weaves an amazing tapestry of biblical, historical, and experiential reflection. Everyone who reads this deeply poetic and accessible theological gift will grow and be strengthened."

—**Cheryl Townsend Gilkes**, sociologist, womanist
scholar, and ordained Baptist minister

"With the power of a Sunday sermon and the insight of a thought-provoking lecture, Dr. Yolanda Pierce's *The Wounds Are the Witness* calls readers to attend to the scars and faithfulness that have shaped the Black experience. Pierce gestures us toward honoring the sacredness in our collective journey toward wholeness. This profound and accessible book is a must-read for anyone looking to heal from pain and keep the faith!"

—**Drew G. I. Hart**, associate professor of theology
at Messiah University and author of *Who Will
Be a Witness?* and *Trouble I've Seen*

"Navigating both pain that is visible and all the hurt that lingers beneath the surface, *The Wounds Are the Witness* holds suffering with care and intimacy. Especially attentive to the ways people rush to 'healing,' Dr. Yolanda Pierce instead bears powerful witness. With unflinching clarity she names a litany of wounds, the searing truth that scars proclaim."

—**Benjamin Perry**, author of *Learning to Cry: Why Our Tears Matter*

"Too often Christian leaders sacrifice theological depth for blithe encouragement. This is a book for Christians who have considered leaving the church when superficial theology is not enough. Yolanda Pierce helps us to hold the pain of this world together with the light and hope of Christ. In a time when critiquing the church is as common as attending it, Yolanda Pierce draws us back to the faith that sustained our ancestors, the faith that was, for many of us, our first love. With unparalleled theological insight and scriptural wisdom, she reconnects us to the spiritual might of the Black church and provides fresh sustenance in our modern context. This is a book to savor and return to again and again."

—**Chanequa Walker-Barnes**, PhD, psychologist, theologian, and author of *Sacred Self-Care* and other books

"With the precision of a pathologist, Yolanda Pierce poignantly parses the painful progression of racial harm. With the profundity of the prophets, she heralds the hope of healing for our weary and wounded souls. A must-read."

—**Michael W. Waters**, pastor, professor, and award-winning author of *Stakes Is High: Race, Faith, and Hope for America*

"Dr. Pierce's latest text, *The Wounds Are the Witness*, supplies the kind of balm that can make attentive readers whole and undergird their work of justice. It contains incisive narrative analysis and displays her deft theological stewardship of the womanist tradition. As one of her former students, and like so many of her readers, I deeply appreciate how her scholarship and Christian witness shine through in every paragraph."

—**Rev. Andrew Wilkes**, PhD, co-pastor, Double Love Experience; author, *Plenty Good Room: Co-creating an Economy of Enough for All*

THE
WOUNDS
ARE THE
WITNESS

THE WOUNDS ARE THE WITNESS

BLACK FAITH WEAVING MEMORY
INTO JUSTICE AND HEALING

YOLANDA PIERCE

Broadleaf Books

Minneapolis

THE WOUNDS ARE THE WITNESS
Black Faith Weaving Memory into Justice and Healing

29   28   27   26   25   24   1   2   3   4   5   6   7   8   9

Library of Congress Cataloging-in-Publication Data

Names: Pierce, Yolanda Nicole, author.
Title: The wounds are the witness : black faith weaving memory into justice and healing / Yolanda Pierce.
Description: Minneapolis : Broadleaf Books, [2025] | Includes bibliographical references. | Identifiers: LCCN 2024020475 (print) | LCCN 2024020476 (ebook) | ISBN 9781506485331 (print) | ISBN 9781506485348 (ebook)
Subjects: LCSH: African Americans--Religion--History. | Church history.
Classification: LCC BR563.B53 P53 2025 (print) | LCC BR563.B53 (ebook) | DDC 277.30089/96073--dc23/eng/20240609
LC record available at https://lccn.loc.gov/2024020475
LC ebook record available at https://lccn.loc.gov/2024020476

Cover image: © 2024 Getty Images; Handstitched patchwork cloth/1468902718 by KrimKate
Cover design: Broadleaf Books

Print ISBN: 978-1-5064-8533-1
eBook ISBN: 978-1-5064-8534-8

Printed in China.

I believe I'll testify.

First giving honor to God who is the head of my life . . .
Protocol demands recognition of those gathered in the
house.

*And to the Bishop, Pastor, First Lady, and mothers on the
Mother's Board . . .*
You express gratitude for another day's survival.

*I thank God that my bed was not my cooling board, and
that my cover was not my winding-sheet . . .*
You acknowledge the injuries this world inflicts and how
God is still keeping you.

*God woke me up this morning clothed in my right
mind . . .*
You offer praise about a grace that is sufficient for your
needs.

*I'm so grateful for a reasonable portion of health and
strength . . .*
And when you are ready, you share the hurts and the pains,
the woundedness and the sorrows.

*But sometimes I feel like a motherless child, a long way
from home . . .*
You trust that the congregation can hold the weight of
your grief and loneliness.

*Nobody knows the trouble I've seen. Nobody knows my
sorrows . . .*
The only answer is to pray your way through it.

It's me, it's me, it's me, O Lord, standing in the need of prayer. Not my brother, not my sister, but it's me, O Lord, standing in the need of prayer . . .

You proclaim hope and healing before they ever come.

Because can't nobody do me like Jesus. Can't nobody do me like the Lord. Healed my body, and told me to run on . . .

You rest in God's justice, for either this world or the next.

And I know there is a balm in Gilead, to heal the sin-sick soul . . .

And somewhere a child is listening, learning, gathering the language she will need to hide in her own heart for a day yet to come.

Precious memories, how they linger . . .

—Yolanda Pierce

*For all the poets, priests, and prophets
bearing witness in the most unlikely of places . . .*

CONTENTS

SETTING THE TABLE
AN INTRODUCTION

I

If you are silent about your pain, they'll kill you and say you enjoyed it.

—Zora Neale Hurston

I learned a set of skills growing up in a storefront church in Brooklyn, New York, not the least of which was breath and voice control. In a storefront church, you learn how to use your big outside voice when reading the scripture, and you learn how to use your quiet voice when the Holy Spirit falls heavy over the congregation. You learn how to use a mic, both how to hold it and adjust it, but also how close or far away you need to be for optimal speaking range. And you learn how to conserve your singing voice, since you are likely to sing for several hours on any given Sunday and multiple other days in a week.

1

We who grew up in storefront churches didn't even know we were being taught to live in harmony with external noise. The sounds of ambulances, car sirens, loud people at the corner bodega, and honking horns formed a musical backdrop for the choir singing or the Hammond B3 organ playing. One year, while rehearsing our Christmas play amid the cacophony of crying younger siblings and bored older siblings, the church elders kept exhorting a group of us kids to "speak up!" We had to use our big voices, they told us, so as to be heard above the ambient noise. Or as one deacon told us, "You have to speak louder than the crying babies."

In terms of volume and pitch, I don't know if there is a noise louder than a crying baby—a baby who really, really wants to be heard and tended to with food or attention or comfort. When I became a parent, it came as a revelation that my tiny six-pound daughter could make her needs known from every room in the house, no baby monitor needed. How something so little could be so loud remains a great mystery to this day. Yes, you develop a mother's intuition for every tiny whimper and coo. But those loud wails of real hunger or distress could scarcely be ignored by anybody in the house. In church, I've experienced the dueling sounds of the preacher preaching and a baby wailing, both trying to express their heart's deepest pangs. The preacher with the mic usually wins as the contrite parent tiptoes out of the sanctuary to the nursery or even outside the church building.

What I learned in that storefront church, and what I learned in the early years of parenting, was that raising your voice above the noise is a necessary life skill. In a world filled with competing sounds and voices all vying to be heard, the ability to make yourself and your needs known is no easy task. But the consequences of not doing so are severe. People will mistake your silence as an affirmation that all is well in your world or that all is well with your soul. When writer Zora Neale Hurston suggests "if you are silent about your pain, they'll kill you and say you enjoyed it," she is speaking of the personal and historical consequences of not elevating the needs of those who are in pain. People will assume that you are no longer hurting, that your pain is long past, and that the harm you endured no longer has any repercussions. When you are silent, people will forget that you've been injured and that your pain is real.

Yet it is a risk to raise your voice above the noise. It's a risk to write about the racial wounds and trauma this nation has inflicted and is still inflicting. The risks run in many directions. You risk being ignored by those who wrongfully think they already know the full story of racism in America. You risk hurting those who share wounds that are still tender and healing. You risk being seen as someone who makes a spectacle out of Black pain and suffering. And you risk being misunderstood by those who are dismissive of the faith that has sustained "many a thousand," as the hymn "The Old Ship of Zion" reminds us.

But to be silent is to risk that stories will be forgotten, root causes of pains will be ignored, and extraordinary moments of healing will go unrecognized as a provision of God's justice. As a womanist theologian—one who reads the biblical text through the lens of Black women's experiences and wisdom—I believe our stories are too important to forget, and I have set myself to the work of a particular kind of memory. For wounded people, landscapes, and communities exist not only as a legacy of traumas and harms but as evidence of the undeniable power of memory and the unstoppable quest for justice.

When the wounds bear witness, the world can never claim ignorance of another's pain. When the wounds bear witness, there is awe and wonder at the capacity for laughter and joy even in the midst of sorrow. When the wounds bear witness, they tell the truth about both the extent of the injury and the extraordinary work of healing.

II

Whatever future ministry I might have as a priest, it was given to me that day to be a symbol of healing. All the strands of my life had come together. Descendant of slave and of slave owner, I had already been called poet, lawyer, teacher, and friend. Now I was empowered to minister the sacrament of One in whom there is no north or south, no black or white,

no male or female—only the spirit of love and reconciliation
drawing us all toward the goal of human wholeness.
—PAULI MURRAY

There is no more sacred ritual I perform within the church context than serving communion. It is a duty I do not take lightly. I relish the opportunity to preside over the table and invite others into a moment of remembrance and reflection. Whether in the most modest of sanctuaries or in the grandest of buildings, standing before the people with unleavened bread and a cup of wine (or grape juice, as in my own tradition) is a humbling act.

I often think about lawyer, activist, poet, and priest Pauli Murray, the first African American woman to be ordained to the Episcopal priesthood in 1977. After completion of her training and ordination, she celebrated her first Eucharist at the Chapel of the Cross in North Carolina. Murray read from the Bible that had belonged to her enslaved grandmother, Mrs. Cornelia Smith. And Murray read the liturgy from a lectern that had been given to the church in memory of the slaveholder who had once *owned* her grandmother.

On that occasion, and in that place, by presiding over the Eucharist, Murray wove together the various strands that had connected much of Black life. These same strands are present for me not only when I administer the sacrament of communion but as I write these words. Those strands were present in my book *In My Grandmother's House: Black Women, Faith, and the Stories We Inherit*, and they are present in this one. These threads include a deep and abiding faith, memories of the ancestors and forebearers, the presence of the bruised and battered, and the ever-present possibility of healing and justice. In the chapters to follow, we will weave together beautiful words of scripture with the realities of Black life in America and the healing capacity of memories—threads that exist in spaces of both harmony and contradiction.

Pauli Murray embraced the contradictory space she occupied. She could touch the tangible items that represented both the enslaver and the enslaved, even as she spoke from a text that was used to justify both slavery and abolition. She stood at the table, breaking new ground as a newly ordained priest, yet also as someone who spent most of her career seeking justice for the marginalized in secular courts of law. She evoked the body of Christ broken for all sinners, even as she had represented those wounded by American racism. And somehow, this contradictory space was one of healing for Murray, one that she said is "drawing us all toward the goal of human wholeness."

When I stand behind the table, calling the gathered community to remembrance, I call forth *all* their sacred memories: those connected to the biblical text and those that emerge from their own lives. In that divine moment and in this one, I take seriously the exhortation in 2 Peter 1:13: "As long as I live in the tent of this body," I will call the people to remembrance. And we cannot remember the healing justice of God without remembering the wounds of the crucified. This is the task of every Christian believer as well as our greatest eschatological hope. It's summed up in the words of my ancestors: our souls must "look back in wonder" at the trauma and also at the healing.

And so we do this in remembrance of the Holy One, who was and is and is to come. The Holy One, whose divine presence accompanied a people across an ocean and is with us still. The Holy One, whose name has never ceased to be whispered by motherless daughters and fatherless sons.

We do this in remembrance of the bruised and the battered, the wounded and the broken. Those whose names will never be known, whose spilled blood was not redemptive, and whose injuries may take a lifetime to heal.

In remembrance of the warriors for justice, the table turners, and the freedom riders. Those prophets who stood outside the gates of the city and declared the Word of the Lord. Those poets who penned indictments against inhumanity and degradation.

In remembrance of those who have experienced justice delayed and justice denied. Those whose sadness has yet to turn to joy, and those whose weeping has endured for more than one night.

In remembrance of the courageous healers, the storytellers, and the midwives. Those who have ushered both words and people into life and unto death. Those whose hands have soothed furrowed brows. Those whose hands have prepared the dead for burial in a potter's field.

In remembrance of the cross and the lynching tree. In remembrance of death and the grave. In remembrance of the resurrection and the ascension.

We are all welcome at this table, whether with visible wounds or unblemished flesh, in the radical belief that only God's justice quenches our thirst, heals our spirits, and renews our hearts.

As the officiant to a time of communion, a sacred fellowship, and as the author of a book about wounds, I set the table and welcome whosoever will to come. I mourn for the hard and painful stories that I must share of the bruised and battered. I rejoice in the triumphs of those who made a way out of no way.

But most importantly, as I preside over the table—in a clear and strong voice, aiming to be heard above the distracting background noise—I remember that both the living and the dead are yet speaking. Together with the writer of Deuteronomy (32:7), we "remember the days of old; consider the generations long past. Ask . . . your elders, and they will explain to you."

1 CARRYING THE BONES
WOUNDED REMAINS

I

> *But to the Negro, when he embarked upon these shores, America to him was a valley: a valley of slave huts, a valley of slavery and oppression, a valley of sorrow. It was a valley of dry bones.*
>
> —C. L. Franklin, "Valley of the Dry Bones"

Bones tell stories. They testify. And bones keep speaking generations after death.

There is a subfield of archaeology known as osteobiography. This term was coined in 1989 by forensic anthropologists Frank P. Saul and Julie Mather Saul, who argue that some of the most significant details of life are embodied within human bones, particularly the skeletal remains of the dead. The word *osteobi-ography* means "life written on bones." Thus osteobiography is a method of doing history whereby bones sketch out the story of a person's health, work, life experience, and social status.

When my enslaved ancestors weren't allowed to speak—when their history wasn't considered worthy of recording—their recovered bones found a way to speak, to testify. Their bones can give us a fuller account of not only their lives but of this country's history and the ongoing cost of generations of genocide.

In Portugal, archaeologists discovered the bones of 158 humans in a trash pit. Genetic analysis confirmed the bones in the mass grave were the bones of enslaved Africans, with sufficient archaeological and historical information to confirm their enslavement. This site, in the Valle da Gafaria, is one of the oldest mass graves of enslaved Africans to be studied, with the location dating to the sixteenth century, the very beginnings of the transatlantic slave trade. Ellen Chapman, the bioarchaeologist connected to the project, remarked, "This site is an incredibly disturbing one, and one that clearly illustrates the pervasive mistreatment of enslaved people by the architects of the transAtlantic slave trade. . . . This skeletal collection is indicative of the high mortality associated with slave ships and the Middle Passage."

The bones recovered at this burial site and others throughout Europe, North America, and South America indicate years of brutal labor, bone-breaking injuries, and starvation. Many of the major arm and leg bones bear evidence of breaks and fractures that were never allowed to heal.

Under the direction of Michael Blakey, an African American physical anthropologist, the site currently known as the African Burial Ground in New York City was excavated. These bones from the eighteenth century were painstakingly labeled, cataloged, and packaged. Examining the remains, Blakey and other researchers found evidence of enlarged muscles and torn ligaments, defects in tooth enamel caused by malnutrition, and unhealed fractures. The skeletal remains also indicated that close and interpersonal violence was common; centrally located injuries near the head, neck, and torso were most likely the result of abuse. Upholding the bioarcheological evidence from across the globe, the bones in New York confirm that these enslaved persons had been worked, literally, to their deaths.

Bones tell the truth of the bodies they have held together and tried to protect. History may fail to tell the story, but bones do not lie.

In Genesis 50, Joseph makes the people of Israel promise to carry his bones out of Egypt, the land of their enslavement, and into Canaan, the land of God's promise for their liberation. Moses is ultimately the one who fulfills this pledge, carrying the bones of his forefather to fulfill the words of Joseph, who had declared: "God will surely come to your aid, and then you must carry my bones up from this place" (Exodus 13:19).

Through a miraculous series of events, God delivers the Israelites from bondage, and Moses is able to bury the remains of his ancestor on free soil. Shechem, the site where Joseph's bones are buried, becomes not just a tomb but a site of remembrance and celebration for his descendants. The very place itself is a reminder that God delivers people. God keeps promises.

When I read about the care and regard that Joseph's descendants showed toward his bones, I think about my own ancestors who endured a reverse exodus—a passage from places of freedom and belonging to a place of bondage. Forced to make this involuntary journey and delivered into the hands of their captors, my ancestors endured the Maafa: the horror, the disaster, the decimation of enslavement that began with the transatlantic journey of the Middle Passage and endured for centuries. When I read about the biblical Joseph, I meditate on my own ancestors' bones, including the millions who perished on this voyage. I think of the millions and millions of their bones that line the ocean, a grim testament to this horror.

In her poem "atlantic is a sea of bones," poet Lucille Clifton writes that her ancestors' bones are "connecting whydah and new york, a bridge of ivory." Her poem links the historical Kingdom of Whydah, a location on the West Coast of Africa in current-day Benin, with New York by way of ancestral bones. The idea of a bridge of ivory haunts me. It is a poetic representation of the shocking number, the millions upon millions, of enslaved who died during these ocean voyages. Whole bodies of the sick and dying, the dead and the disabled, the disobedient and the defiant, were thrown overboard.

Over the course of time, the ocean strips away the flesh, the muscle, the sinews, and the tendons. The ocean receives whole bodies and leaves behind bleached bones. The Atlantic Ocean is as much a valley of dry bones as it is a watery grave. Like shipwrecks that sink to the ocean floor, carrying their secrets with them, bones in the ocean are saturated with human history.

My spirit is heavy when I ponder the weight of this history. Bones in the ocean. Bones in unmarked graves. Bones broken and unhealed. Bones discarded and unremembered. Life is written on all these bones. Whole histories of peoples, civilizations, and families are written on these bones.

The story of the prophet Ezekiel in the valley of the dry bones is a beloved narrative of preachers everywhere. I've heard some of the best sermons imaginable on this story of the prophet's vision: an eschatological resurrection of the dead, restored to life by the breath of God.

But where that valley is located—and whose bones are dry and in need restoration and new life—depends on the preacher. For African American preacher C. L. Franklin, father of the legendary Aretha Franklin, the valley was this very nation. When "white Europeans came to this country, embarked upon these shores, America to them was a land of promise, was a mountaintop of possibilities, was a mountaintop of adventure," Franklin said. But to the enslaved and their descendants, America was "a valley of dry bones." In his sermon on this beloved Ezekiel text, Franklin so beautifully sums up the significance of the "bridge of ivory." The voluminous ocean itself can be a valley, a chasm, and a pit from which one requires divine intervention.

In Ezekiel 37:3, God asks Ezekiel directly: "Son of man, can these bones live?" As a womanist theologian, I petition God with my own questions as I read this story. Can the bones of my ancestors live? Can the bones of my ancestors be resurrected from the watery grave? From the black hole of historical amnesia and deliberate disregard? Where is my Shechem, my site of remembrance, to mark this bridge of ivory? Can those memories and stories and traditions and faiths and family lineages that were drowned in the ocean ever live again?

When God asks the prophet Ezekiel "Can these bones live?" Ezekiel does not answer "yes." Within the Christian tradition, Ezekiel is considered one of the major prophets, along with Jeremiah, Isaiah, and Daniel. We understand these men to be gifted with unique insight from and intimacy with Yahweh. So Ezekiel's lack of an affirmative answer when asked whether God can do something that seems impossible is no small matter. Doesn't he believe that God can restore life to dead things?

Instead, Ezekiel answers: "Sovereign God, you alone know." I find Ezekiel's honesty refreshing. He doesn't assume that he knows the answer. He doesn't know whether the dead can live again. Despite being a prophet, he doesn't strike a self-confident posture in his response to God. Instead, Ezekiel humbly acknowledges what he does not know: certain matters of life and death are above his human understanding. Ezekiel's response to God acknowledges God's sovereignty and also his own humanity.

And that is the only response I can give when, heavy in spirit, I consider this bridge of ivory. Only God knows if fractured bones can be knit back together. God alone knows if the wounded can be made whole. Only God knows if the stories, cultures, and histories—written on bone and buried deep beneath the ocean or discarded like trash—can ever live again.

II

This is now bone of my bones and flesh of my flesh.
—GENESIS 2:23

One of my favorite haunts as a young mother was a huge bookstore that had a play area for children. Incorporated into the children's book section, it was a large and open space, carpeted, with small tables and chairs just right for small humans. There were Lego tables and train stations at the perfect height for busy toddlers. It was a place of a child's unfettered joy: wide open spaces and new toys and books. I spent many late afternoons in this bookstore, in awe of my own ever-growing daughter, incredulous that she was no longer one of the tiny little bundles in a stroller, and yet longing for the day she would want to read quietly by herself in the corner.

One quiet Tuesday afternoon, I saw an elderly couple in the corner of this play area. At the very end of the section usually occupied by nursing mothers, a very frail man was sitting next to an equally frail woman in a wheelchair. If their white hair and wrinkles were any indication, this was a couple of many years, easily in their eighties or nineties. The elderly man had a small pile of children's books on his lap. In a surprisingly firm voice, he read *Brown Bear* and *Goodnight Moon* to his companion. Between stories, he would pause and gently touch her hair or wipe her face. He held her hand, and he'd only let go long enough to turn pages or switch books.

The woman was motionless and silent. Part of her face drooped, perhaps from a stroke, but her eyes were clear and focused. As the man read *Pat the Bunny*, a touch-and-feel book, she moved her hand over the different textures. For over an hour, without wavering, he read to her the books that you could imagine they had once read to their children.

There are no words to describe the look in the eye of this man or his tender care. The woman in no way appeared a burden to him. He smiled at her as he read; he laughed at the funny places in each book, and the love in his eyes could be seen across the room. He attended to every comfort of his silent, still companion. And when the pile of books was finished, he simply sat, sometimes holding her hand and sometimes lightly patting her knee. He described to her the action of the busy toddlers, and he murmured sympathetically when a new little walker took a tumble. He lovingly patted the head of one bold crawler who found his way to the couple's feet. But in all of this, he was ever present. She was the center of his joy.

Those of us in the children's section that day were witnesses to this love made plain. We could not help but be moved by this display of devotion, tenderness, and faithfulness. It was a silent demonstration of a commitment and compassion that I no longer believed existed in this world.

At some point, a granddaughter or other caregiver came along and ushered this lovely couple out of the store. As I bundled up my daughter, negotiating a stroller, diaper bag, and work tote, I noticed that my parenting burdens felt lighter. The glimpse of unconditional love at the end of life somehow made it a bit easier to feel the joys of the unconditional love I had for my own baby beloved.

On the way out the store, a sampler near the marriage books and wedding gift section caught my eye. The words "flesh of my flesh, bone of my bone" were embroidered on a small hanging quilt. When watching an elderly man read children's books to his female companion, I was witnessing this sentiment in action, this verse made incarnate.

Flesh of my flesh, bone of my bone: that verse in Genesis 2 was never meant to be a scientific treatise on biological sex difference or human evolution. Nor was it meant to establish a gender hierarchy. Instead, it is a metaphorical description of how a loving God can knit together two souls with a love so powerful that I am still compelled to write about it twenty years after witnessing it. To be of the same flesh and bone is to share a connection that transcends time and our human understanding.

All of us are knit to ancestral connections we cannot comprehend. We are compelled to remember and share the stories of a people, time, and place centuries before our own, which we have never known but to which we are connected by flesh and bone. Just as the ancient tales of biblical characters reverberate in my spirit, the love story of an elderly white couple I observed from afar touches my soul. I was a twentysomething Black woman with a newly crawling toddler; my social context and life circumstances could not have been more different from the couple I observed. And yet, their obvious love story and deep devotion still exist in my memory. I know this elderly couple from twenty years ago is no longer alive, but I remain a living witness to their faithfulness.

I long for the dry bones of my ancestors to be made flesh again through acts of memory. I yearn for their love stories and survival stories to be cherished as a part of our historical recollection. Even across differences in age, place, and circumstances, I want there to be an identification with the humanity, dignity, and perseverance of my own forebearers, whose very existence is a witness to God's keeping power.

III

But his word was in mine heart as a burning fire shut up in my bones.

—JEREMIAH 20:9 (KJV)

Hundreds of years, perhaps more than five hundred, pass between Joseph's initial request to his descendants to carry his remains to freedom and when he is finally, permanently, laid to rest.

In Genesis 50, Joseph makes his family pledge to carry his bones out of the land of their bondage and enslavement. Upon his death, he is embalmed according to Egyptian custom and buried. Then in Exodus 13, over four hundred years after Joseph's death, Moses disinters the bones and carries Joseph's remains with the children of Israel as they begin their extended journey to the promised land. It isn't until Joshua 24, long after the death of Moses and the assumption of the mantle of leadership by Joshua, that Joseph's bones are finally laid to rest in a home that had been promised to his family many generations earlier. Finally, after half a millennium, Joseph rests in peace, his memory a blessing to his descendants.

This story is a lesson in faithfulness, both of humans and of God. A community was faithful to a five-hundred-year-old promise, and God was faithful to deliver people into liberation.

Yet what became of these bones between Joseph's death and his burial? I am intrigued by what modern science reveals about the decomposition process. We now know that over time, depending on the circumstances, even a material as hardy and durable as bone can fade away. While Joseph had been likely buried in an expensive sarcophagus, his coffin was removed and exposed to the elements for a very long period. Given this fact, the Israelites may have carried more dust than bones from Egypt to Shechem as they slowly moved from life under the Pharoah to Canaan. While we speak of Joseph's bones, it may very well have been granules and fragments that were ultimately buried in Shechem. From dust we have come and to dust we shall return.

The bones of my forebearers too—bones that create a bridge of their own across the Atlantic Ocean—have likely disintegrated since the Middle Passage. Three factors determine the rate of decomposition of bones: time, temperature, and the environment. We have known for a long time that our flesh is fragile.

Now we know that even the hardiness of solid bone cannot defeat the ravages of time, significant shifts in the temperature, and the environment.

Knowing this, I marvel at a God who chose to take on the frailties of humanity, becoming flesh and bone, to walk with us among the earth: fully human, but no less divine. To understand the Incarnate God is to grapple with both divine humility and divine power. It is an act of humility to enter the world as a helpless infant, completely dependent on imperfect human love for your survival. It is an act of power to take on the fragility of bone, flesh, sinew, and tendon and yet defeat death.

Time, temperature, and the environment: over time, with the optimal temperature and the perfect environment, bones can last thousands or even millions of years. Fossils are just buried bones that contain tiny air pockets reinforced by mineral deposits. These mineral deposits can preserve the shape of the bone structure for millennia. But rarely are the conditions optimal for the preservation of human remains. In the ocean, oxygen levels, acidity, microbial activity, and scavengers can make quick work of human bones. On land, skeletal remains are subject to decomposition based on many variables, including length of time to burial and exposure to air, heat, and cold. The scientific term for the process whereby bones decompose is known as bone diagenesis. The literal translation of *diagenesis*, from the Latin, means "across generations" or "through creation."

These weighty words force us to consider how, across a great expanse of time and throughout all creation, we are to handle the bones of our ancestors. The question for me is not how we physically care for their literal bones. The question is how we will handle the inheritance they have bequeathed.

The story of Joseph's descendants carrying his remains is not about the bones themselves but the remembrance. Joseph did not want his descendants to forget their earlier circumstances, even when their current situation had significantly improved. After all, what does freedom mean if centuries of bondage are forgotten?

Joseph's physical coffin, and whatever remained inside, were the physical reminders that God sets the captives free. The inheritance of these remains changed his ancestors. They remembered God's promise. They remembered God's provision. They remembered God's warning to turn away from false gods and to only worship the one true and living God.

We also must remember. I am compelled to bear witness, to put some flesh on the stories, songs, triumphs, and tragedies of my people.

There is no August 1963 March on Washington for Jobs and Freedom, with over 250,000 people in attendance, without an acknowledgment of the August 1619 arrival at Port Comfort, Virginia, of "twenty and odd Negroes," who were sold and resold on the shores of the New World. There can be no recognition of the 2009 inauguration of President Barack Obama that doesn't grapple with the 1857 *Dred Scott v. Sandford* decision by the Supreme Court, which ruled that people of African descent "had no rights which the white man was bound to respect." And there can be no celebration of the institution of the contemporary Black church that fails to struggle with the truth of James Baldwin's indictment: "When the white man came to Africa, the white man had the Bible and the African had the land," but now, the African no longer has the land and is being "forced to digest or to vomit up the Bible."

These examples are painful truths, but they also deepen our understanding of the beauty and triumph of survival. In remembering our wounds, we go against the calls of many who say we must "stop dwelling on the past" and "move on." To remember these beautiful struggles is to counter the national impulse to remove Black history from public schools on the grounds that it makes people uncomfortable and sad to learn about the origins of the Black presence in the United States.

But willful amnesia is never God's plan. The sacred scripture is filled with commands to *remember*. Remember the terror of slavery. Remember the pain of genocide. Remember the horrors of being without a homeland. The ancient peoples of the Bible are mandated to honor their ancestors and transmit a community's history from generation to generation, with all its pains and joys. And alongside these human memorials is the remembrance and worship of a God whose steadfast love endures forever. A God who is with us in slavery and freedom. A God who is with us as we involuntarily cross an ocean or willingly cross the desert.

If tradition is the "handing down of the fire and not the veneration of ashes," as Gustav Mahler says, then the holy lesson I have learned from the bones of my ancestors is clear. Even if I can never recover the ashes, dusts, and fragments of their physical bones, I carry within me a fire I can never allow to die. It is the fire of justice and faith that compelled Harriet Tubman to return multiple times to free others from enslavement, insisting they choose to either live free or die. It is the fire of hope and faith that caused Bayard Rustin to fight for an end to racial discrimination in employment, organize freedom rides, and help plan the March on Washington—despite being barred from speaking at the march because he was gay. It is the fire of audacity and faith that propelled Mary McLeod Bethune to open a school, and then a hospital, where neither had existed before, to educate and heal those living under the yoke of Jim and Jane Crow.

My faith, my ability to hope and dream, rests solely on my belief that death does not have the final say. We carry the bones, but they do not define us. In that magnificent passage from Ezekiel, God gives Ezekiel an assignment: to prophesy to the dry bones in the valley. In the face of so much death, Ezekiel is told to simply speak. He is called to speak life into a dead situation. Suddenly, miraculously, bones lock into place. Breath fills the dead. In those death-dealing situations in which all hope is gone and no hope for new life appears, Spirit-breathed words become flesh. Can the healing of our own wounds begin with words of life and hope, with words of tenderness and love?

I may never be able to recover the bones of my ancestors that comprise that bridge of ivory. But these memories and their impact are like fire shut in my bones. The bones of that great cloud of witnesses may have long decomposed, but the fire of their faith is still present. Like the prophet Jeremiah, I can't keep this news to myself. The words of the beloved spiritual say it best:

> *Said I wasn't gonna tell nobody, but I*
> *Couldn't keep it to myself . . .*
> *Couldn't keep it to myself . . .*
> *Couldn't keep it to myself.*
> *Said I wasn't gonna tell nobody, but I*
> *Couldn't keep it to myself,*
> *What the Lord has done for me.*

We sang this song at the 2018 funeral for Dr. James Cone, arguably one of the most important, and one of the earliest, scholars of Black theology. The words of this song are referenced in the title of his posthumously published memoir, *Said I Wasn't Gonna Tell Nobody: The Making of a Black Theologian*. Even after Cone's death, his work is still reminding readers to speak life into death-dealing spaces. He is still challenging us to remember the power of our words to triumph over the grave. And like the ancient Israelites carrying their ancestors' physical remains, we are called to carry the theological and historical bones of our people.

Like fire shut up in our bones, the stories flame up and shout. They testify.

2 WON'T BREAK MY SOUL

THE WOUNDS OF SHAME

I

Therefore have I set my face like a flint, and I know that I shall not be ashamed.

—Isaiah 50:7 (KJV)

During the summer of 2015, policer officers were summoned by a call about noise at a pool party in McKinney, Texas. The footage of this incident of police brutality, shot by some of the teenagers at the party, shows one white police officer throwing a Black teenage girl wearing only a bikini to the ground. He repeatedly slams her face into the grass and forcefully straddles her while thrusting his knees into her back and neck. The same officer pulls out his loaded service revolver and points it at the other Black teenagers who are guests at the party.

Videos from this event went viral. As all these traumatic incidents do, this one descends from a long history. The McKinney pool party conjures up a protracted and ugly racial pattern in which white people have called police on Black people engaged in minor infractions or for no simply reason at all. White privilege allows white people to use the police as a private security firm of sorts—a defense against perceived threats of blackness. And so whether it's birdwatching in the park or showing real estate to a client, Black people know that if a white person assumes that they don't belong in a particular place, police brutality may ensue.

The racial dynamics of this particular community were also laid bare. The west side of McKinney, where the pool and this community were located, is an almost entirely white, affluent community; it's the location of major commercial development, high-end retail, and multimillion-dollar homes. The town was deliberately split by the North Central Expressway. The east side of town is home to communities of color, poorer neighborhoods, and government-funded affordable housing. As African Americans watched the video, many of us remembered the way those in power in our own hometowns or cities had deliberately built train tracks, highways, and other infrastructure to maintain racist and segregated housing. In wealthy, white neighborhoods like the one where this incident took place, Black teenagers are often assumed to be interlopers from literally "the wrong side of the tracks."

The pool itself also troubled those of us who watched this incident and its aftermath. Swimming pools have long been sites of racial tension and police brutality in the United States. In cities like Cincinnati and St. Augustine, white people poured bleach and threw nails into swimming pools to prevent and protest the desegregation of these spaces. Race riots took place at pools in Baltimore and Washington, DC during the 1940s. Pools were a particular site of racial animosity because of the white fear of Black men assaulting white women in this intimate environment, along with white people's racist beliefs about the dirtiness and disease they thought African Americans harbored.

So during the summer of 2015, millions of us viewed footage that revealed both police brutality at a pool party in Texas and the long history of racism in our nation. We were dismayed at the presence of twelve white police officers brutally restraining a group of Black kids enjoying a pool party.

In that moment, before I could process this history as either a scholar or theologian, I was a Black woman and mother. I watched as a young teenage girl in her bathing suit, her not-yet-grown, delicate body, was physically assaulted, straddled by a large armed man, slammed into the ground while her assailant pulled her hair. Unknown to me, tears were streaming down my face as my mind tried to process everything this video showed. The mother in me, the woman in me, was praying fervently:

Please, God, don't let her bathing suit top slip,
Please, God, don't let her have to endure nakedness,
in addition to assault, in front of this large group of strangers.
Please, God, don't let her naked adolescent body be viewed,
again and again, on the news and on Instagram reels,
as she is tackled to the ground.

In those few seconds, as I was trying to process what I was seeing, another white man entered the frame of the video. He was not in a uniform, and he was coming to the aid not of the child crying on the ground, whose body was buckled under a grown man's knee in her back. Apparently a civilian, the man attempted to aid the armed police officer in restraining someone who was already being handcuffed.

At this point, tears gathered under my chin, and I felt the sting and the heat of anger and shame. My anger is easy to understand, and it was widely shared by millions of Black and Brown and white people who watched the video. Empathy, too, came quickly to Black and Brown viewers of the video; many of us had the capacity to identify with her situation, to know that in a different context, that could have been us or our children. I am she and she is me.

Black women viewing this video were mostly united in equal parts horror and shame. Articulating why we felt shame on behalf of a girl we did not even know is hard. The feeling of shame runs beyond empathy, and it may seem to others that shame is the last thing any Black people *should* feel when we watch police brutality unfold on our screens. Marginalized and oppressed people often feel ashamed of what happens *to* them; there is shame felt for the wounds inflicted on them by someone else. Rationally, you would think that shame would lodge itself in the hearts of the ones causing the harm. Violent law enforcement officers who brutalize the unarmed *should* feel ashamed. But far too often that shame is felt and internalized by the victims and survivors and their extended communities.

This teenager, certainly, had done nothing for which she should feel ashamed. On a warm Texas day, she was being a kid, hanging out with her friends and listening to music at the pool. There, something terrible and life-altering happened *to* her, through no fault of her own. If anyone should feel shame, it's the police officers and the white man who voluntarily joined their number. The shame should be felt by those who watch this video with the purpose of sharing with others, exploiting her body for sensation and spectacle.

The shame I feel is the sting of humiliation on behalf of a barely dressed child I fear could be even further violated by those paid to serve and protect the public. The shame is connected to the long-standing history of Black women's bodies being unprotected and undefended. The shame is about the spiritual, psychological, and physical assaults on the spirits, minds, and bodies of too many other Black women, myself included, that go unreported, unseen, unacknowledged, and unknown. The shame is about the lack of control and agency over your own identity, about the way that technology, in a time of white supremacy, turns us all into voyeurs of racialized suffering. Even when you attempt to avoid the images and videos, they are broadcast again and again. Were I to name this young woman in these pages, you could go online and encounter photographs of her half-clad body pressed to the ground. These are the only images online that appear connected to her name.

What do we do with the wounds of the spirit due to humiliation and shame? Can we remain unmoved and unbowed by the physical and spiritual blows in a world that wants to break our spirits? Do we harden our face like flint, becoming resolute, unmovable, and undaunted in a world of racial or social hierarchies? How do we deal with the deliberate personal and public attempts to shame, to humiliate, to make an example of those who are most powerless to defend themselves?

Beyoncé sings ever so triumphantly, "You won't break my soul." But this world attempts to break the souls of so many that it becomes difficult to even imagine a salvation for those wounded in spirit and in body. What does hope look like for those whose bodies are pressed to the ground by a knee? What does hope look like for those whose dead children are left on the ground for four hours while helicopters and news crews hover above? What does hope look like when white supremacy has you feeling ashamed of being abused instead of being angry at your abusers?

II

> *Then Miriam the prophet, Aaron's sister, took a timbrel in her hand, and all the women followed her, with timbrels and dancing.*
>
> —Exodus 15:20

If you are a child growing up in a Holiness-Pentecostal church, you learn how to perform every function in the church, early and often. You will sing in every choir or praise team. You will serve on the junior usher board as soon as you are big enough to stand still at the door, with a starched white blouse and white gloves. You will help clean pews and set up microphones. You will be called up to give an Easter speech or recite a Christmas poem. You will be asked to stand on the step stool they bring out especially for you so that you can recite the Sunday's scripture from the big pulpit Bible as soon as you learn to read. And if you have any musical ability at all, you will play the drums or keyboards or even the bass guitar when you are barely tall enough to reach the instruments.

I grew up in such a church, and in the space of those wooden pews, which were lovingly dusted and polished by the church mothers, my gifts were affirmed and room was made for my talents. The elders told me I had a good, clear speaking voice, so I was called upon for every reading or speech. Because of their encouragement, I thought nobody could read scripture or give an Easter speech better than I could. The trustees told me that I was smart, and they allowed me to count the coins from the offering with them. Because of their trust, I became a careful custodian of my own tiny allowance. The church mothers told me I was a good teacher, and they sent me to teach the younger children when I had barely hit puberty. Because of their love, I learned even more scripture and theology. Week after week and year after year, this congregation told me that I had a multitude of gifts, and like they did for all the children of the church, they gave me space to explore them all.

What apparently I could *not* do, in a church in which kids did a little bit of everything, was carry a tune. My lack of singing ability was a shock to the grandparents who raised me. Both my grandmother and grandfather had excellent singing voices, and each played various instruments. My grandfather, a preacher, had a short-lived professional singing career before he became a minister. My grandmother played the piano by ear, and the sounds of hymns and spirituals filled our home. When I was a toddler, I was promptly placed in the choir, the Sunbeams, like every other church kid. I eventually graduated to the junior choir, and I just assumed that one day, when I was an adult, I'd join the young adult choir. Everybody in my childhood church sang, and everybody at home in my Black neighborhood or who attended my Black public schools sang too.

And so one day during choir rehearsal at church, when I was told to sing a solo for one verse of a particular song I knew very well—one of the staples of our church—I didn't hesitate. Church kids do all the church things, and singing is just one of them. And that's when I really heard my own solitary singing voice for the first time. Not the voice surrounded by other strong and beautiful voices. Not the voice blending in with the gospel albums my grandparents played at home. Just my own voice and the piano.

And I sounded terrible.

To their credit, everyone else must have known this already, because no one winced or flinched or reacted at all. But I went home determined to practice my little solo and get it right. I sang my verse again and again, while my grandmother patiently played the piano. At some point I looked at her, perplexed as to why everything sounded off-key when I sang it but so beautiful when she or others sang this same song. She saw the baffled look on my face and, with the wisdom of her years, simply said, "I think you would be great on the tambourine."

With that, she handed me a child-sized tambourine that I didn't even know we had. Almost every pew at our church had a tambourine, and some people brought their own tambourines to church each week, carrying them in a special tambourine bag along with their Bibles. Tambourines appeared during testimony services and tarry services and during Sunday morning worship and Saturday afternoon rehearsals. I had never picked one up to play because there were already so many talented women, young and old, whose tambourines caused the church to rock. Every Sunday, it was as James Baldwin describes his own childhood church: "There is no music like that music, no drama like the drama of saints rejoicing, the sinners moaning, the tambourines racing, and all those voices coming together and crying holy unto the Lord!"

So my grandmother handed me this small tambourine, and instead of singing my short solo, I fell into its rhythm. I had apparently absorbed the ability to play tambourine by osmosis. So in the coming years, I played that tiny child-sized tambourine until at some point I graduated into a full-sized adult one. I continued to sing in the choir, my voice and tambourine harmonizing with the other members. No solo was necessary (or ever requested of me) again.

I still ponder how so many of my grandparents' musical gifts managed to skip over me, but I also take solace in the fact that I play a mean tambourine. In most of the sacred spaces I now occupy personally and professionally, the congregation may politely clap or sing along with the choir, or they may lift a hand or two in praise. But every once in a while, I need the racing tambourines, the moaning, the foot stomping, and the holy cries of my youth to feel that I have really been to church. I still long to see men and women dancing in praise to the holy noise of clapping and tambourines.

It is only with an adult's deep gratitude that I can appreciate a space that never shamed me for what I couldn't do well, never humiliated me for my failures, and also managed to extract gifts I didn't even know I had. Not a single soul told me that I sounded like a hoarse frog when I sang. No one told me that I missed a line in my Easter speech or that I didn't correctly pronounce "Methuselah" or "Melchizedek" when I read the scripture. I didn't know as a child that the trustees had already counted the coins. Or that the adult ushers had to work even harder on the Sundays the junior ushers were in charge. I was simply aware that I could try anything in this church and it would be a safe space to land.

So it grieves my spirit that so many churches, so many religious spaces, have been sites of humiliation and shame for individuals and groups. I mourn that a place that taught a little Black girl that she could go to a college no one had ever seen before is the same place that tells someone else they are going to hell for who they love or who they marry. I lament the private and public humiliations suffered by those whose truths and identities are mocked from the pulpit. I grieve with those whose humanity, vocational calling, or salvation seems under debate by way of narrow-minded sermons and poor biblical exegesis.

The hot sting of shame in your cheeks and your chest, that feeling of humiliation that settles into the pit of your stomach: these are far too common experiences in churches. I've heard people shamed from the pulpit for what they were wearing or how they styled their hair. I've listened as ministers shamed the poor or those with addictions. I've grieved as pastors humiliated single mothers and unmarried women in sermons from behind the sacred desk.

These hierarchies, in which those with power and privilege—or those who simply wield the microphone—shame and blame others and reinforce their "superior" social standing, diminish the radical equality God promises in places like Galatians 3:28. These hierarchies fail to recognize that we are all one in Christ Jesus and that our work as Christians is to exalt God, not to shame our neighbors.

As a theologian, I am forced to reflect on the many ways our institutional churches shame instead of save. I must sit with the complexity and contradiction that a place of affirmation for me has been a place of shaming and defaming for others. I grieve that a place that loved me and propelled me to a rich, full life has been a space of condemnation and castigation for others. Too many have been metaphorically pushed in the dirt, stripped bare, and humiliated in sacred spaces by those leaders and laity who police the tradition and set themselves as the enforcers of religious orthodoxy. The tools of shame and humiliation break the soul. The tools of shame and humiliation weaken our capacity to be witnesses to God's saving grace and compassion.

III

Miriam sang to them: "Sing to the Lord, for he is highly exalted. Both horse and driver he has hurled into the sea."
—EXODUS 15:21

Miriam is the first woman in the Hebrew Bible to be named a prophet. We initially encounter her when she is in the process of saving the life of her baby brother, Moses. The pharaoh has issued a decree to kill all the newborn Hebrew boys. Moses's mother Jochebed has placed him into a waterproof basket she wove, and she has set him afloat in the Nile River. As a child encountering this story, I was deeply interested in the role of Miriam, a big sister like me.

It is Miriam who is sent to watch the basket containing baby Moses and Miriam who dares to tell the pharaoh's daughter that she knows exactly the right person to serve as a caretaker for the infant. It is Miriam who fetches her mother, who is then both reunited with her infant son and paid to be his nurse. The Hebrew midwives, Shiphrah and Puah, have likely helped to usher Moses into the world, and Jochebed has given birth to him and now nurses him. But it is Miriam, the elder sister, who saves baby Moses from a certain death.

Along with her brothers Aaron and Moses, Miriam becomes a leader and prophet to the people of Israel. When their Egyptian captors drown in the Red Sea, she leads a song of triumph along with Moses, calling forth the women to dance and play instruments in praise of the God who delivered them from slavery. Miriam sings, she leads a group of tambourine-playing women, and she ushers her community into a season of rejoicing. Everything in the biblical text suggests that Miriam is a revered and capable leader, called to serve alongside her brothers.

So I struggle mightily with a story in Numbers 12, in which both Miriam and Aaron confront Moses about his Cushite wife. A brother and sister confront a sibling, but only the sister is shamed and punished.

Whether Miriam and Aaron's concern is that their brother's new wife is Cushite or if there is another reason for this confrontation, the text does not say. We simply know that the brother and sister approach Moses about his marriage. And then, as recorded in Numbers 12:2, Miriam and Aaron dare to raise a second issue: "Has the Lord spoken only through Moses? Hasn't he also spoken through us?"

God, angry at Miriam and Aaron, rebukes them for daring to ask this question, and then inflicts Miriam—and Miriam *only*—with spontaneous leprosy, a contagious and debilitating skin disease. God confirms Moses's favored status, and Aaron is left untouched. Miriam alone bares the physical wounds of this confrontation.

My womanist hermeneutic of suspicion flares into full effect with this passage, and I have questions. Aaron and Miriam were in fact called to lead besides Moses (Micah 6:4), so why would she be punished for speaking with authority? Why is Miriam punished with leprosy, a disease that was so shameful in the ancient world because of its visibility and contagion, and not some other private affliction? Why does a woman—the first one to be named as a prophet—face divine punishment for speaking and not the man alongside her, who is asking the very same questions?

Some commentators suggest that Miriam must be the primary instigator of these complaints since her name is recorded first; that must be why she is punished while Aaron walks away without a blemish. On that particular issue—who is the instigator of this encounter—the text is silent. But even if she is the instigator, that does not diminish her shame and humiliation. In addition to the stigma of her disease, Miriam is also cast out of the camp for seven days. These days away from the camp are only granted as a result of Aaron's prayer for mercy and healing for his sister. But lest we think that being away from her people during this time somehow lessens Miriam's shame, we have to remember this: to be cast outside of the camp in the ancient world meant going without shelter or protection from predators and the weather and perhaps even access to food and water.

When I think about how Miriam is shamed, I can't help but consider how many women are shamed by someone who decides to "take them down a peg or two" because they perceive women as too loud, or too powerful, or too audacious. In this familial trio of leaders, the hierarchy and patriarchy are maintained; only the woman, the female "instigator," has to be humbled for daring to voice that God has also called her.

Our culture loves to shame women by framing humiliation as a corrective or a preventive to arrogance and pride. And humiliation is a form of domination, as the powerful try to maintain control of both the narrative and their position. Can we imagine Miriam being used as an example, particularly to other women, of what happens when one dares to question the expected order of things? For daring to ask a question, she is shunned and cast aside. She bears on her body the marks of a warning to others: this is what happens when you transgress authority.

The civilian in McKinney, Texas, who assisted the armed police officer in restraining a young teenager, tried to keep those so-called uppity Black children from thinking they could come into a white community. This civilian felt so empowered in his whiteness that without even asking if help were needed, he "assisted" the police in upholding his perception of the law. By actual violence, Black children are being told to "know their place" in this racist hierarchy, a lesson reinforced by handcuffs and drawn weapons.

Likewise, fire-and-brimstone sermons against queer or trans persons are a form of rhetorical violence and domination, with the goal of humiliating and belittling those brazen enough to believe that they, too, have access to God's grace. The tools of shame and humiliation are wielded by those who fundamentally don't believe that God's surpassing love is sufficient for all made in God's image and likeness.

The story of Miriam, Moses, and Aaron in Numbers 12 concludes with the one redemptive note: "and the people did not set out on the march until Miriam had been brought in again" (Numbers 12:15 NRSV). In my divine imagination, it is a group of women—perhaps a group of the most vulnerable among them, perhaps those with their own marks and scars—who insist that the people cannot move forward without Prophet Miriam. Instead of leaving her behind to fend for herself, continuing without her during this long march from slavery to freedom, these walking wounded insist on waiting for their prophet and spiritual midwife. Instead of expecting Miriam to eventually catch up with the rest of the camp, the people stay in that same place until Miriam is restored and returned to her rightful place in their community as one of their prophets. I imagine the tambourine-playing women rejoicing when Miriam comes back home.

And here is the holy lesson that I have learned: there is no progress unless the wounded among us—those broken in heart and bruised in spirit—have space to tell their stories and share their burdens. Justice is only possible if the ones cast outside of the camp, the city, or the church are lovingly brought back into a changed and transformed community. The discarded and forsaken must be given the lead if we are to move forward in building God's beloved community. Justice is only possible when we reject the sinful impulse, as Malcolm X describes it, to hate the people who are being oppressed and align ourselves with the powerful, the ones who are *doing* the oppressing. Justice is only possible when you are offer a towel and a helping hand to a vulnerable young girl instead of assisting with the handcuffs.

If Beyoncé is right, and she often is, we build a new foundation for justice and love by releasing the power of the tools of shame and humiliation used by those who try to break our souls. After all, is it progress if we leave the most vulnerable behind?

3 DOWN SOUTH
HEALERS WITH WOUNDS

I

Jesus saith unto him, Rise, take up thy bed, and walk. And immediately the man was made whole, and took up his bed, and walked: and on the same day was the sabbath.

—JOHN 5:8–9 (KJV)

The members of Generation X may be the last generation of urban Black children who were routinely sent "down south" during the summer. We may be the last large wave of city kids whose formative years were shaped by extended periods of time in the rural South, in segregated communities. Now that I am a parent, it boggles my mind to think about the logistics of these summer visits—about who made the arrangements and how these traditions were organized. The level of coordination involved in just arranging summer day camps for my own daughter took a laptop, cell phone, insurance cards, reams of paperwork, and the same intellectual effort it took to write my dissertation. Yet somehow families in the 1980s created an entire plan for multiple children to travel several states away, for weeks and weeks at a time, with only a tattered address book and rotary phone.

The kinship networks that enabled this tradition had largely disappeared by the time my own child was born, and today, it would seem unfathomable (and borderline illegal) to put unaccompanied children on a Greyhound bus and ship them off to a distant relative for an entire summer. But for many of us 1980s babies growing up in the inner cities of New York, Philadelphia, and Chicago, going down south during the summers was just what we did. With nothing more than sandwiches in brown paper bags in our hands, we were shipped South, fully trusting that, on the other end of a six-to-ten-hour bus ride, a trusted adult would meet us.

Down south: those two words were always used together, as if down wasn't enough to indicate a southerly direction. Going down south conjured up a sense of return. Of home. Families who had traveled north during the Great Migration and had lived in major urban cities for decades still considered the South home. Our family reunions took place down south despite the fact that almost everybody in the family now lived within a few miles of Brooklyn. For four weeks, six weeks, or even more, young cousins from different branches of the family tree found themselves on ancestral southern land. Sent to North Carolina or Georgia or Virginia, we'd be put under the care and supervision of a great-aunt, or somebody's grandmama, or whichever older family member was willing to take in a ragtag group of city kids for the summer.

This time was magical and bewildering, everything familiar and unfamiliar at the same time. We were fed our usual grits or oatmeal for breakfast, but they tasted different in North Carolina. We consumed gallons of iced tea, which we knew and loved, but we were frustrated by the amount of time that sun tea took to make and why it needed to sit in the sun. We learned how to shell peas and to wash collard greens. I was fascinated by the garden in the front yard that yielded food we could eat immediately. And I was mesmerized by my great-aunt's bed that was so big and tall and soft that I needed a step stool to climb into it.

As enchanting as that time was, I was also truly a city kid, with little tolerance for the never-ending heat and constant presence of bugs. Mosquitoes were the bane of my existence. And while my relatives tried to convince me that the bugs singled me out because I was so sweet, I knew the bugs targeted me personally because I was an outsider. The older boy cousins mercilessly teased the youngest of us, bringing frogs and turtles into the house, knowing that a bunch of city kids found these to be scary and alien creatures. The heat was so oppressive that even the most recalcitrant among us succumbed to a midday nap or quiet time in front of the television. Southern heat was a different level of heat—so hot that even the hardiest of my boy cousins gave up on their outdoor adventures and sought the shade of the house. If we had been back in New York, we would have stayed outside and played all day; we would have found a fire hydrant to cool us off and continued our games of tag or double Dutch even in the heat of the early afternoon.

I will never forget one summer afternoon of sitting on the front porch with my great-aunt. We were waiting for the temperature to settle somewhere slightly below the fires of hell when a cousin came limping back to the house with serious cuts from whatever the boy cousins did all day. My great-aunt gently cleaned his scrapes and bruises as best she could. But one stubborn cut would not stop bleeding.

What happened next I can still see in slow motion, every detail burned into my memory. My great-aunt reached up into the inner corners of the rafters of the front porch, pulled down the delicate strands of a spiderweb, and pressed the silken threads directly on my cousin's still-bleeding skinned knee.

I was speechless. A spiderweb as wound care? The only familiarity I had with spiders came from my reading of *Charlotte's Web*.

That there were spiders just casually living outside the house, and that they could have anything to do with healing, fascinated me. Where were the Band-Aids like the ones my grandmother used to tenderly dress my own scrapes? Only my upbringing in the strictest of households, in which children did not question adults, kept me from asking everything that raced through my brain. Mosquitoes and frogs and spiders and random insects I could not name were bad enough. But to actually take the *web of a spider* and put it on a clean wound? It challenged even my seven-year-old imagination. My cousin's knee stopped bleeding almost immediately, and he ran off, surely to continue whatever dangerous activity had injured him in the first place.

If I had had the words or courage to express what I had witnessed, I would have asked: "What manner of place *is* this?" To be honest, that was the question I wanted to ask about much of what I encountered during my summers in the rural South. We ate unfamiliar fruits and vegetables from mason jars; rarely did any food come from store-bought cans. My boy cousins pointed out critters like skunks and bunnies and opossum that only existed, as far as I was concerned, in cartoons on television. The first time I saw a deer munching in my great-aunt's well-tended garden, its beauty rendered me speechless. In this rural North Carolina town, a bunch of city kids were given aloe vera and cod liver oil. We were fed way too much, never gained an ounce, and still outgrew our summer clothes. We slept despite the overwhelming heat, the white noise of the standing fan stirring around the dusty air, and yet we slept better than we ever slept. We went to rural churches where the pastor only came once a month because he had four different churches under his charge, none large enough to sustain a full-time pastor.

At the end of the summer, we were sent back to New York and Philadelphia and Chicago with healthy skin and full bellies and the requisite dozen or so mosquito bites. We were sent back on a Greyhound bus, our suitcases now packed with canned preserves and vegetables in clear mason jars.

Even as other memories from my southern summers would fade, that summer I returned to Brooklyn with a memory, vivid and intense, of a spiderweb that could heal a wound.

II

A spider's web is stronger than it looks. Although it is made of thin, delicate strands, the web is not easily broken.
—E. B. White, *Charlotte's Web*

One afternoon almost two decades later, I was sitting in a study carrel in a university research library, trying my best to finish my doctoral degree. I was wishing for a reprieve from the relentless cold and lake-effect snow, knowing that none would be forthcoming until I finished my dissertation.

I was researching what had become my greatest intellectual passion: the spiritual lives and theology of enslaved persons. I was immersing myself in narratives written by those who had endured enslavement and yet also managed to write about their spiritual lives and their theological understandings. Research is like detective work in that one detail leads to another, which leads to another. In this case, in a series of one-citation-leading-to-another events that could have only been ordained by the Holy Spirit, I found myself reading an article in a medical journal. That article described cutting-edge research on the healing properties of real and artificial spiderwebs used for wound care. Immediately I was back on my great-aunt's porch, watching incredulously as she grabbed the spiderweb from the rafters of her porch and dressed my cousin's scrapes.

The medical journal in front of me described the ancient application of spiderwebs in healing and their documented usage since at least Roman antiquity. I read about the coagulant vitamin K and its role in treating cuts and burns. I learned about the natural antiseptic and anti-fungal properties of spiderwebs, as well as their tensile strength and adhesive flexibility. Several paragraphs detailed the way that pharmaceutical companies are developing medical products based on spiderwebs: products for burn victims, diabetics, and cardiovascular patients.

Nothing in that article, however, addressed the reason I was filled with such wonder. Because before the medical journals, before the peer-reviewed research, and before the pharmaceutical trials, men and women living close to the land knew how the leaves and the trees and the plants were all for the healing of both people and the nation. They trusted that a Creator who had made everything had provided for them, through the natural world, all that was needed for survival and thriving.

My great-aunt, a descendant of enslaved persons, carried healing knowledge that had been passed down to her over generations, and she was still practicing that knowledge in this rural North Carolina town. Enslaved women handed down cooking and medicinal practices that had nurtured and protected their loved ones. Generations of rural Black women born free, in the same towns and former plantations where their own grandmothers had been enslaved, kept these traditions alive. Herbs and roots and leaves and plants could relieve suffering, cure certain illnesses, help to safely deliver babies into this world, and help prevent other pregnancies from occurring or coming to full term. In the oppressive, dangerous, and dehumanizing realities of chattel slavery, when Black life had very little value except for its function as labor, Black women served as cooks, herbalists, and healers and helped others survive.

While these traditions are often dismissed as "folk medicine," I take seriously the vast array of innovative sources these women employed to counter the death-dealing forces they routinely encountered. They spent their lifetimes helping to heal the wounds of others, even as they themselves were routinely brutalized and dehumanized. These women delivered babies even when their own children had been stolen. They ground bone marrow for anemic babies even when they themselves went hungry. They made healing salves and painkillers to relieve the discomfort of even those who brutalized them. They gently tended to the wounds of unruly boys who could barely squeak out a "thank you" before heading back into danger.

I was among the millions of children raised on *Mister Rogers' Neighborhood*, the children's education show that aired on public television. Even my saved, sanctified, Holy Ghost-filled, and fire-baptized grandparents couldn't find anything wrong with a show that taught children to be kind. The host of the show, Fred Rogers, was an ordained Presbyterian minister who told children to "look for the helpers" when times are scary. "You will always find people who are helping," he said, and that advice makes sense to me as a theologian. God is present where there is kindness, goodness, and gentleness. Thinking about that article and my memories of my great-aunt and other women in my family, I now urge people to "look for the healers" when you want to see where and how God shows up in the world.

Look for the healers . . . those working on the physical, psychological, spiritual healing of others. Look for the healers . . . those who are gently working to knit together fractured people, fragile families, or even broken institutions. Look for the

healers . . . those who, even with their own burdens, work to create spaces where the wounded can be heard without judgment or
condemnation. Look for the healers . . . those who value consent
and tenderness in a world where so much touch is violent and
malevolent. Wherever the wounded are being made whole, in
body and mind, the Spirit of the Lord is. Look for the healers,
and you will see the hands and feet of God.

Swiss psychiatrist and psychoanalyst Carl Jung is credited
with popularizing the term *wounded healer*, drawing upon an
ancient archetype: the healer has wounds that need care even
as he is treating and healing others. While the patient is being
cared for, that act of caretaking is also healing and nurturing
the healer. In his work *The Wounded Healer: Ministry in Contemporary Society,* Catholic priest and theologian Henri Nouwen
extends the idea. "Who can save a child from a burning house
without taking the risk of being hurt by the flames?" Nouwen
asks. "Who can listen to a story of loneliness and despair without taking the risk of experiencing similar pains in his own heart
and even losing his precious peace of mind? In short: 'Who can
take away suffering without entering it?'"

Nouwen points us toward a life in which we are called to
be like Jesus and enter into the suffering of others. As he writes:
"Jesus is God's wounded healer; through his wounds we are
healed." Like many theologians, Nouwen centers the act of *suffering* as identification with Christ. As a womanist theologian, I

find it important to center the act of *healing*. In other words, the wounded healer is not simply a vessel for suffering. Instead, he or she is a *healer with wounds*: someone with agency, power, and autonomy, despite the wounds and the suffering. It is not the presence of wounds or the depth of his suffering that define Jesus's power and authority; it was his divine ability to heal, to set free, to repair, and to restore. By keeping our focus on the healing, we don't sanctify the suffering or valorize the harm. The suffering isn't holy; the One who heals, who is the source of our salvation, is.

At the very center of Jesus's earthly ministry is the act of healing, again and again. Jesus healed those around him on at least three levels: the physical, the psychological, and the spiritual. In John 5:8, Jesus says to the man at the pool of Bethesda, who had been suffering for thirty-eight years, "rise, take up thy bed and walk" (KJV). This man's physical body is healed, and his health is immediately restored. He is now strong enough, despite a lengthy illness, to take up the very bed mat to which he had previously been confined, to walk away from a place that had been his prison.

In Mark 5, when Jesus heals a woman who had been bleeding continuously for twelve years, he doesn't merely restore the proper functions of her physical body. Jesus calls this unnamed woman "daughter," a term of tenderness and endearment. This naming is an act of psychological healing. The woman's physical condition rendered her unclean and untouchable in her own community, even to her own family. By healing her body *and* by calling her daughter, Jesus gives her a new social identity. She is no longer the woman with the "issue of blood," defined by her sickness and confined by her deficiency. There is psychological healing in being named as a daughter, joint heir, and beloved child of God. It is as restorative as the physical healing she experiences.

And in Mark 5, Jesus heals the man from Gerasene who had been tortured by his demons; this man had been chained, isolated from others, and spent his days cutting himself with stones. After being healed by Jesus, the man's restoration is complete; he is seen clothed and restored to sanity and wholeness by those who had previously shunned him. But more importantly, this man has a spiritual transformation, as he travels to the Decapolis region to tell others about Jesus and becomes what is often described as the first apostle to the gentiles. Jesus heals him physically and also spiritually; the evil spirits were cast out of him, allowing room for the indwelling of God's pure and holy Spirit. When we have received spiritual healing, our souls long to tell the good news of the One who has redeemed us.

When we study the healing miracles of Jesus, they offer dramatic proof of God's intervention in the world. Healing is an act of personal restoration but also an act of radical social reconstruction. When we look for the healers, we see that an individual is healed, yes. But we may also notice that the family, community, and nation who are witnesses to the healing are also being transformed. Witnesses marvel at those who have been healed, and many also choose to place their trust in such a compassionate and tender Healer. By lovingly caring for the disabled body, the hemorrhaging body, the diseased body, the nonambulatory body, Jesus replaces the neglect and societal inattention and community abandonment with divine dignity.

There is a beauty and simplicity to how Jesus healed the sick, the wounded, and the broken. There were no complicated rituals or recitations of arcane words. There was no exchange of money or complicated build up to the healing act. People simply came to Jesus with their unmet needs, and he healed them. I cannot help but recall the simple and uncomplicated way that my great-aunt placed the spiderweb on my cousin's knee, a gesture she had clearly done before. My cousin implicitly trusted that she could help him. Like the miracles that Jesus performed, tenderness and trust were always at the center.

III

As he drops deeper and deeper into the abyss, slowly his eyes begin to pick up the luminous quality of the darkness; what was once fear is relaxed and he moves into the lower regions with confidence and peculiar vision.

—HOWARD THURMAN, *THE LUMINOUS DARKNESS*

Spider Woman, also known as Grandmother Spider, is a creation goddess in many Indigenous American cultures, including the Mayan, Pueblo, Hopi, and Navajo. Grandmother Spider is characterized as a wisdom keeper, a nurturer, a protector, and a mother to humankind. Grandmother Spider is a healer for her people and for the earth. When people tell stories of Grandmother Spider, they ascribe value to her role as a sacred thinker and the founder of culture, not just as the bearer of children. According to Laguna Pueblo poet Leslie Marmon Silko, Grandmother Spider was "Thought Woman," and she "named things and/as she named them/they appeared." This creation goddess spoke and named an entire universe into existence.

Learning about Grandmother Spider has given me language to describe why my great-aunt's healing work, and that of others like her, was so meaningful to me. These women had garnered secret knowledge from years of study, observation, experience, and faith. They were creators and healers. Through research, trial and error, and their own forms of peer review, they used the humblest of plants or food or material substances to bring health to and improve the quality of life of those they loved. These alternative knowledges and alternative economies allowed people to survive genocide and enslavement and segregation. Like Grandmother Spider, these women named things, and they appeared.

These knowledge systems, with a focus on healing and restoration, represent a counternarrative to the dominant story: that the traditions of rural southern folk were ignorant, unscientific, and based on superstition. Contemporary scientific validation of centuries of healing work has forced us to take another look at knowledge we discarded. The easy dismissal of the ways of poor folks, of the value and the benefits of how they lived, along with the wisdom they practiced and the healing strategies they deployed, is now being reconsidered in the light of empirical evidence. But the aunties and abuelas and curanderas and rootworkers have long cultivated both their faith and their healing arts without external validation. My great-aunt trusted God, and she trusted her years of experience when caring for us.

When visiting my relatives in rural North Carolina, I also learned to trust the relentless darkness. My great-aunt knew the healing properties of darkness, too, long before most people knew that science confirms that darkness is good for us. There were no streetlights and barely any light from neighboring houses. At night, the weight of darkness initially felt heavy and scary for a city kid with an active imagination, who was used to the lullaby of honking car horns and police sirens. The first few days of each summer, I'd struggle with the quiet and the darkness. I remember the last summer I spent in the rural South, an angsty tween desperate even for just enough light to read a book, hearing my great-aunt remind me to simply be still. There is healing in the darkness, she said. Darkness is just as important for us as light.

Science now confirms that there is physical healing that can only happen when we sleep; there is restoration that takes place in the darkness of night. Only when it's extremely dark, without the presence of blue light from cell phones and televisions, can your body produce the hormone melatonin, a natural substance that has anti-inflammatory, antioxidant, and anticoagulant properties. Scientists believe that most of us are no longer getting enough darkness. Artificial light from devices, lamps, and car headlights pierce even the darkest nights. Light pollution has become as devastating as air pollution for both people and the environment. The rhythms of human biology evolved before artificial light, allowing our bodies to take advantage of both bright days and dark nights. Very rarely do those of us living in densely populated areas encounter dark nights anymore. Our eyes rarely have a chance to practice our natural night vision. We are missing the deep sleep that occurs in total darkness, and we are missing the ways our natural reflexes develop in darkness.

We also suffer from weak theological language that associates evil with darkness, which is a devastating link. In our theological laziness, we use words like *darkness* or *dark deeds* when we are actually trying to express ideas about sin or evil. We have incredibly rich language we could use to express moral failings that don't rely on a light–dark binary, but we take shortcuts that do more harm than good. Creation required darkness. God called the light *day* and the darkness *night*—and pronounced *all* of it as good. In Exodus 20:21, "Moses approached the thick darkness where God was." In Psalm 18:11 (KJV), David describes how God "made darkness his secret place; his pavilion round about him were dark waters and thick clouds of the skies."

This is the "luminous darkness" that theologian Howard Thurman describes as a place where God dwells. It is a place of provision and protection. As the psalmist says: "Surely the darkness shall cover me; even the night shall be light about me" (Psalm 139:11 KJV). Some healing, protection, and provision can only happen in the thick darkness where God dwells. Like the impossible vastness of space, this thick darkness is a place that inspires awe at its sheer existence.

Redefining the meaning of darkness provides a counter-narrative to the anti-Blackness that is so pervasive in much of Christian theology. We love sharp binaries, and life seems so much simpler if darkness equals evil and light equals good. We want the bad guys dressed in black and the good guys dressed in white. But our metaphorical language often becomes literal, and we move quickly from metaphorical darkness as an expression of evil to actively thinking about dark people as evil. We fear the literal darkness of night, while closing our eyes to the reality that some of the most infernal acts are committed in broad daylight. We fear the dark Other invading our neighborhoods and homes, while most harm is experienced at the hands of our very own families.

We need to recover the transformative power of darkness, just as we need to recover the traditions, ways, and beliefs of our elders. In both, we can find beauty and possibility. The Jesus who spits in the mud and makes a paste from his saliva to cure a blind man is the same Jesus who got up to pray at night, enveloped by the darkness. The holy lesson that we who have been wounded know is that God can use the simplest of things—mud and spiderwebs, sun and tea, sleep and darkness—to bring healing and life for those who believe.

"To know the dark, go dark," poet, essayist, and novelist Wendell Berry says. The luminous darkness is where God dwells. It's where spiders spin healing silk and where bodies find restorative sleep. When we travel in the dark, Berry assures us, we may learn that the darkness itself "blooms and sings."

LAY ASIDE EVERY WEIGHT

4 THE HEAVINESS OF WOUNDS

I

You wanna fly, you got to give up the shit that weighs you down.

—Toni Morrison, *Song of Solomon*

In her 1977 novel, *Song of Solomon*, Toni Morrison builds upon long-established legends that some enslaved Africans escaped the horrors of bondage by physically flying away. Countless stories, memoirs, and oral traditions describe captured Africans who flew off slave ships to return to Africa. And there are tales of enslaved African Americans who simply flew away from the labor and brutality of chattel slavery on American plantations.

In her novel, which is set in the 1960s, Morrison uses the songs and chants of children's games as subconscious memory of this long-enduring recollection of supernatural flight. No one takes the pastimes of children's play seriously. But revered and remembered within their hand-clapping and jump-roping games are stories of people who could fly.

In almost all of the folktales of Flying Africans, to "fly away home" is to return to the continent of Africa, the land of the ancestral roots and origins of people of the African diaspora. Africa was home even if the person who took flight had never been there. Morrison's novel pointed me to the oral stories maintained by the descendants of Igbo Landing in St. Simons Island in Georgia. There, in 1803, a group of seventy-five captured Africans took control of their slave ship and then, refusing to submit to the bondage that awaited them on shore, walked into the marshy waters. Some first-person accounts called this act suicide, believing that those captured were choosing death over whatever fate awaited them in Georgia. Other first-hand accounts insisted that the people flew.

In graduate school, I read the testimonies of formerly enslaved persons interviewed by the Federal Writers' Project in the 1930s and 1940s, who testified to having watched men and women take flight. In *Drums and Shadows: Survival Studies among the Georgia Coastal Negroes*, I encountered the stories of the descendants of slavery who described miraculous flights, along with tales of folk medicine, apparitions, and an active spirit world.

As I researched these stories, I could not help but hear the echoes of a song learned in my childhood and beloved by the saints of my Holiness-Pentecostal upbringing:

> *Some glad morning*
> *When this life is over,*
> *I'll fly away . . .*
> *To that home on God's celestial shore,*
> *I'll fly away.*

I had been taught that "I'll Fly Away" is about eschatological hope: that death is not the end for the Christian believer, and that to be absent from this earth is to be present with God. I learned that by and by those who at the end of this frail human life would reach the celestial shore—the pearly gates of heaven—would rejoice. This song fit with all the popular cultural references I had been exposed to about death and the afterlife: angels who fly from heaven and around earth. Incandescent souls rising from the body and flying toward a bright light. In Western Christian mythology, human flight seems otherworldly and supernatural: the soul is torn from the body and heads toward the clouds to a heavenly home of golden streets and angels playing harps, white robes and white wings.

While this particular vision makes for beautiful art and great Christmas ornaments, it leaves me wondering why so much of Christian hope is grounded in the afterlife and in the possibilities of joy only achievable *after* death. Why is home on earth so unpalatable that we long for an unknown celestial shore? And why does some "glad morning" come only after this life is over and not in this present age?

The myth of the Flying Africans sparked my divine imagination as I encountered story after story of living, breathing, thinking human beings deliberately taking flight. The Black folks who took flight were active agents deliberately challenging—and exiting—their brutal circumstances. They took flight toward hope and possibility. Having already experienced the death that was chattel slavery, they flew toward the life they believed awaited them at home in Africa.

As I wrestled with this myth, this song from my childhood, and even the sacred scripture, I was finally able to articulate the theological question for which my soul needed answers: Is there a space for us to fly, to survive and thrive, right here and right now? *Can we soar on earth, in this lifetime?* Can home be an earthbound place where we experience the liberation that comes with flight? Is there a life for us here without the heavy burdens that weigh us down?

With the use of metaphorical flight in her novel, Toni Morrison provides one such possibility for soaring on earth. She insists that those who are heavy-laden can take flight if they are willing to give up the baggage that weighs them down. The main protagonist of the story, Milkman Dead, is able to fly at the end of the novel once he lets go of his pain, bitterness, and self-hatred. Morrison contrasts the successful flight at the end of the novel with the unsuccessful flight (and death) of someone who attempts to fly on the very day Milkman Dead is born. In a full circle moment, it is only Milkman Dead, who spends the entirety of the novel searching for and discovering his ancestral history, who can freely soar.

The Flying Africans can fly because they understand themselves as Africans: members of a community with a history, with traditions, and with a past. They are people with a home to which they can return. They are not objects, despite the weight of their legal definition as such. By shedding their figurative and literal chains, the Flying Africans defy natural order, the laws of physics, and the legal restrictions of slavery.

In public and private settings, and especially after I've lectured on the Flying Africans, people have asked me whether I believe these flying stories to be true. They have challenged me about the veracity of the claims made by formerly enslaved people who insisted that they watched others fly. While people accept the metaphorical use of flight imagery by enslaved and formerly enslaved people, I am inevitably asked how I can present this information so matter of factly. Why would I not add a disclaimer of some kind? A caveat that listeners should take it all with a grain of salt, a reminder that it is all a myth?

Inherent in this question about truth is what weight we give to stories, whether we acknowledge that our stories become our history and our theology. I believe in many orthodox truths of Christianity that defy rational explanation: a virgin birth, Jesus's resurrection from death, miraculous healings. My identity as a believer, the theology of my faith, is constructed from these ancient myths. I believe in a miracle-working, death-defying, way-out-of-no-way-making God.

So the question we should be asking instead of *if* these men and women could fly is this: What does it mean that they believed they *could*? What does it mean that they believed they could take flight despite living in a world that denied their human dignity and legally proclaimed their inferiority? What psychological burdens did Africans and their descendants have to lay down in order to defy their condition of social death and to have sufficient agency to believe they could fly?

This same myth of "flying away home," as echoed in the gospel song, does critical theological work for believers. It reminds us that we must let go of human-made constructs that diminish and degrade. We must throw aside every weight burdening us so that we can experience the fullness of the reign of God on earth, in the here and now. Our burdens, when given to God, become light enough to allow us to fly. We are called to both build the kingdom of God on earth and also to rest on the promise that there is a more excellent place being prepared for us.

The cover of Virginia Hamilton's African American children's book, *The People Could Fly: American Black Folktales*, depicts people in their regular clothes flying into the sky. Most are wearing overalls and the tattered clothing of farmers and sharecroppers. This image of regular folks in everyday clothes, in flight, fuels my own theological imagination, as it provides a distinct contrast to the whiteness of both the people and the clothing usually depicted in images of the heavenly host. The cover of a children's book reminds us that God calls ordinary people, from fields or from offices, to cast our cares aside and build beloved community.

II

> *Can't you see it? Can't you feel it? It's all in the air.*
> —NINA SIMONE, "MISSISSIPPI GODDAM"

I once used Toni Morrison's quotation about the "shit that weighs us down" in a theology lecture. Afterward, someone from the audience came up to me and privately objected to my use of profanity. A curse word was inappropriate in a lecture focused on God-talk, they suggested, and it had tainted my entire lecture.

Part of me wanted to reassure this person that my grand-mother had raised me right and profanity isn't typically part of my vocabulary. I wanted to admit that I had hesitated before including Morrison's quote in my lecture, fearful that I would offend someone. As a Black woman I feel hypervigilant when I speak and when I write, aware that my every word is subject to critique, that every misstep will be judged more harshly than those of my white peers.

So I was just about to apologize when I was struck by the irony of the moment and stopped up short. His undue focus on one single word had caused him to miss everything else I had to say. I had made an intentional decision to use the language Morrison used in her novel to be true to her words and out of respect for her artistry—and because, sometimes, only a good curse word can capture life's essence. I thought of Nina Simone sitting down at the piano on Sunday, September 15, 1963, and composing "Mississippi Goddam," and of how there were no better words to capture the anguish of four young Black girls in Birmingham being killed in a white supremacist terror attack on their church.

My mouth suddenly refused to form the words of an apol-ogy. "Thank you. Duly noted," I said, and that was that.

Later, as I reflected on that conversation and spoke with friends and colleagues about it, I realized that worrying about one four-letter word in a forty-five-minute lecture is *exactly* the kind of petty shit that weighs Christians down. This person was more worried about obscene language than obscene conditions—conditions that cause some people to want to curse God and die. We can be so focused on the small, insignificant things that we don't see truth when it is staring us in the face. We are so weighed down by the inconsequential and trivial that the weightier matters of the law—acts of justice and mercy—elude our grasp. In creating a false dichotomy between the sacred (the holy) and the profane (the ordinary), we fail to see how often the most profane things teach us about the most sacred.

As the speaker, I had drawn on Morrison's words to pose some important questions: What is the excrement, waste, muck, and mire in our lives that keep us from feeling worthy before God? What are the burdens that keep us from loving ourselves and loving the light of God within each person? What are the loads we've carried for so long that their weight has begun to feel like an old, familiar friend?

Humans have an unfortunate habit of mocking or dismissing a question if the answer to it may trouble us, convict us, or indict us. But sometimes the greatest contribution we can make is to ask a piercing question. This was the case with Black theologian William R. Jones in his pivotal 1973 work, *Is God a White Racist?* Some have refused to engage with Jones's book, published over fifty years ago, because of the provocative nature of the question. But by daring to even pose the question, Jones insists we contend with two concepts that we are often afraid to interrogate: (1) practices of racism within Christianity and (2) the justification of racism by Christian doctrine and tradition. By asking the provoking, perturbing question, Jones calls us to think more deeply about our faith, our religious traditions, and our nation's ugly racial and religious history. Some have found the question that Jones asks so profane that they are unwilling to engage the sacred assignment contained within his pages.

The question that haunts me these days is one posed by theologian and mystic Howard Thurman in his 1949 book *Jesus and the Disinherited*. He asks: "What, then, is the word of the religion of Jesus to those who stand with their backs against the wall?" That is: What do the words of sacred scripture mean for people who are in hurting places? What does Jesus have to say to the wounded and the outcast? For those who are among the "least of these," what can this Christian faith provide? Does it provide anything of substance? Is it all talk and no action? Is religion sufficient as a remedy for those who have their backs against the wall, or is it meaningless?

Thurman's searing question prompts deeper, more probing questions of ourselves, of our nation, and of our faith. And there is no guarantee that the answers to these questions will actually bring us closer to God or make us more faithful believers. Our biggest fear is that an honest answer to the question of, "Is God a white racist?" or, "What is religion to those with their backs against their wall?" will shake the foundation of beliefs we thought we firmly held.

In Jesus's few years of earthly ministry, he asked many questions of his followers and his critics. Many of these questions were rhetorical, as the person merely confirmed what Jesus already knew. "What do you want me to do for you?" Jesus asks of the man whose vision he knows needs healing in Mark 10:51. "What is your name?" he asks of the demon-possessed man in Mark 5:9. These questions were meant to benefit the persons being questioned. The questions invite them to declare their needs or the truth of their situations before Jesus intervenes.

More often, the questions Jesus posed were designed to upend long-cherished beliefs and deconstruct traditions and established doctrine. In Matthew 5:46, when Jesus asks, "If you love those who love you, what reward will you get?" he criticizes those who are impressed with their own righteousness. In Matthew 16:26, when Jesus asks, "What good will it be for someone to gain the whole world, yet forfeit their soul?" he challenges the idea that possession of the riches and wealth of the world are sufficient for salvation. And in Luke 10:36, when Jesus asks, "Which of these three do you think was a neighbor to the man who fell into the hands of the robbers?" he dismantles the ethnic, racial, and religious barriers for who counts as our neighbor.

For the Pharisees, Sadducees, and other religious authorities Jesus encountered, these questions were profane speech. Heretical talk. They were quick to accuse Jesus of disrespecting tradition and defying religious custom. But for those released, healed, and set free, Jesus's questions were life-giving and soul-refreshing.

The questions I posed to an audience based on Toni Morrison's words were designed to help listeners name their burdens and figure out a way to lay them down, to give their burdens to God. Those questions were premised on one of the most important questions Jesus asked in John 5:6: "Do you want to be made well?"

Are you ready and willing to take your burdens to the Lord and leave them there? Can you see it? Can you feel what's in the air? Do you believe that you can take flight and soar?

III

"If you surrendered to the air, you could ride it."
—Toni Morrison, *Song of Solomon*

I carry my life around in a large tote bag. It is filled with everything I might need to face the day ahead: wallet, toiletries, papers and books, laptop, umbrella, chargers, water bottle. I am the person who can provide you with medicine if you have a sudden headache or hand sanitizer if you've left yours at home. Need gum or a cough drop? It's in my bag. I never know when I'll have a few minutes of downtime, so I'm always ready to boot up my laptop and return some emails. Or check my phone and return text messages. I feel naked, vulnerable, without a bag of things to carry.

I've carried some kind of book bag or tote bag since kindergarten. I want to be prepared for the unexpected, to be able to pull out of my bag, like magic, whatever is needed for the occasion.

For the longest time, I didn't notice my bag's heavy load or its impact on my body. I liked feeling prepared and in control. I liked that other people knew they could come to me if they had a need. It took a visit to the doctor to point out what should have been obvious. My persistent neck strain was due, in part, to carrying around such a heavy bag for so many years—a bag whose weight I barely felt anymore.

That's what happens with all the psychological baggage, trauma, and burdens we carry: we can get so used to lugging it around that we don't even know how to lay it aside. We no longer notice the strain of the weight we bear. We get so used to the wounds of life, so used to the brokenness, that we don't even realize those things are the source of our physical pain or spiritual suffering. Pain becomes our normal way of being in the world. We can't imagine a life without the heaviness and the despair. We may even wonder who we are without the pain.

And truthfully, we don't even know how to allow God to carry our burdens. Sure, it sounds good. But how can we actually rest in the promise that God's yoke is easy and God's burden is light?

The solution lies in our surrender. I had to give up my heavy tote—my illusion that I could solve every problem that came my way by pulling something out of my bag. I had to accept that my phone may die, that it might rain, and that people could wait for an email from me. I had to surrender my desire to control everything around me and focus on my healing and well-being.

One day, weeks after trading my weighty bag for a cute (and tiny) purse, I turned my head to acknowledge someone standing at my office door—and realized that I no longer felt any neck strain! For far too long, I had adapted my physical movements to accommodate the pain instead of actually figuring out the cause of it. I didn't even know how much pain I was in until after the pain was gone.

Yes, our burdens are real and they are heavy. And surrendering those burdens don't make them magically disappear. But what if we begin with the simple acknowledgment that God is God and we are not?

Some problems we cannot solve with our limited human capacity. Some situations we cannot control. Some wounds cannot be healed with our earthly Band-Aids and stitches. We have to place our hope and trust in the One who promises never to forsake us. We have to admit the vulnerability we feel in even surrendering our burdens to God. We have to confess that we may not even know who we are without the pain that has defined us. And we have to be willing to uncover the source of that pain, even if that means facing our own sins and transgressions.

We sing the precious hymn "I Surrender All," but we struggle to live out the lyrics. I have learned this holy lesson: surrender is an everyday process of admitting our human frailty and the Divine's sovereignty; it means to ever love and trust God and in God's presence daily live. Surrender is a posture of our empty hands lifted up, our unburdened arms extended to God as if we are preparing to fly away home. Our ability to thrive, to ride the air, comes not because we deny the burdens we carry or the heavy load we have. Our hope rests in the One whom even the winds and rains obey. Our trust in God, who has promised to be our burden bearer, has to be deeper than all those forces that weigh us down.

THE SOIL IS EXHAUSTED AND SO AM I

THE WOUNDS OF CREATION

I

> *But when ye entered, ye defiled my land, and made mine heritage an abomination.*
>
> —JEREMIAH 2:7

Large jars of soil stand in row upon row upon row of wooden shelves. They are loamy, sandy, chalky, silty, peaty: all the possible textures of soil in the United States. The colors would be beautiful—orange, red, black, brown, ocher—were the story of the soil not so brutal.

Blood haunts these soils. Each jar is engraved with the name of a lynching victim, along with the date and location where the person was killed. Some of the jars are marked *unknown*, signifying that a lynching took place at that location but that details like the victim's name were never recorded. It makes for a sobering tour to see this exhibition. From the red clay soil of Alabama to the deep black soil of Texas, the varying colors are a reminder of the geographic expanse of racial violence in America.

The Equal Justice Initiative has documented the brutal lynchings of more than 6,500 African-descended people between 1865 and 1950. Community volunteers send a jar of soil to the National Memorial for Peace and Justice in Montgomery, Alabama, from a documented lynching site. Here at the Legacy Museum, that jar joins a growing collection of hundreds of other jars of soil from locations of racial terror.

In one way, this soil is all that is left behind of a Black life. Except there are photographs too. There are photos of the white families who cheerfully attended these public executions. They'd attend lynchings literally as picnic outings, with their young children in attendance. They'd strip the lynched persons of their clothing, sometimes even cutting off ears and toes as a "token" of their attendance. There they stand, adults and teenagers and children, in their suit coats and ties and party dresses, smiling.

I cannot unsee the postcards, the photographs, the posed family portraits at these sites of human degradation. I cannot unsee the smiling faces of those who saw themselves as devout Christians. And as a Christian and as a Black woman, I cannot unsee what theologian James Cone writes: "The cross and the lynching tree interpret each other. Both were public spectacles, shameful events, instruments of punishment reserved for the most despised people in society."

As I stand in front of these glass jars, I am overwhelmed by the sheer number of names and dates. What deep sorrow this soil represents, what brutality this very dirt has known. It is a visual representation of spilled ancestral blood, still crying out from the ground. And it makes the lyrics of James Weldon Johnson's poem, later set to music by his brother and known now as the Black national anthem, even more poignant:

> *We have come over a way that with tears have been watered,*
> *We have come, treading our path through*
> *the blood of the slaughtered . . .*

I do not know if any members of my own familial bloodline are represented by any of the named or unnamed jars. I do not know if, while traveling through these locations, I have planted my feet on soil soaked with this violence. I wonder if, as God tells Cain in Genesis, the blood of our family members is crying out to us from the ground. I wonder if soils, like bones, speak.

And I cannot escape the fact that the soil itself, in these very same areas, is utterly, entirely, literally exhausted. Many of the soils of this region are either dead or actively dying due to the hundreds of years of another form of racial violence: plantation slavery.

Soil exhaustion, or *soil fatigue*, is the scientific term for ground that has been so poorly managed that it can no longer sustain crops or other plant life. During the era of enslavement in the United States, particularly during the nineteenth century, unsustainable agricultural practices led to the degradation of the land and soil. Forests were cleared to plant crops, and overtilling the ground for a single cash crop, like cotton or tobacco, led to the eventual destruction of the top layers of soil. This hastened exhaustion and erosion. The focus on a single cash crop depleted the soil because the same nutrients were required year after year, giving the soil no time to replenish the precious sources of its survival.

In his 1836 autobiography, fugitive slave Charles Ball writes about the destruction of the soil by slaveholders: "They are attempting to perform impossibilities—to draw the means of supporting a life of idleness . . . from a once generous, but long since worn out and exhausted soil . . . tortured into barrenness by the double curse of slavery and tobacco." Ball indicts the laziness and idleness of slaveholders who, in order to support their indolent lifestyles, stripped both the soil and enslaved people of life-giving resources. The greed of American slavery and its focus on short-term productivity still impacts us today. In addition to lynchings, the jars of soil at the National Memorial for Peace and Justice represent layers and layers of other horrors: forced removal of Indigenous persons; slavery; sharecropping; and contemporary environmental abuses.

Scientists believe that it takes anywhere from 500 to 1,000 years to regenerate a single inch of topsoil, which is the upper layer of soil that contains the organic matter necessary for plants and crops to thrive. The economic engine of chattel slavery was an environmental disaster. As colonizers pushed westward, they depleted the soil. Eager for more land to exploit, they were insatiable in their willingness to destroy the very land they claimed was a precious gift from God. Manifest destiny—the religious belief that white settlers had been given dominion over the land encompassing what we now call the United States—must always be juxtaposed with the environmental harm done to that very land and her Indigenous peoples. How does one claim the land as sacred and holy while at the same time stripping it of its lifegiving capabilities—and doing it all in the name of God?

The soil of our nation still holds onto the memories, traumas, and wounds of this exploitation. Some land will now always remain barren; species have been forever lost; and waterways are still polluted as a result of the brutal treatment of our nation's natural resources. More than 150 years after the formal end of enslavement, the dirt, the waters, and the forests are still telling the story of systemic abuse and neglect. Enslaved people easily saw the connections between how the soil was being treated and how they experienced bondage. They saw how enslavers treated both them and the land as cheap, disposable, and exploitable resources, of which there seemed to be a never-ending supply.

If the very dirt is still telling a story, and if there is land on which we still cannot plant crops and topsoil because it is in recovery, why can't we imagine that the very bodies of the descendants of the enslaved are also still telling a 400-year-old story? If the soil is still exhausted, still trying to heal from its depletion and devastation, can we imagine of the collective exhaustion of those who penned lines like "God of our weary years / God of our silent tears" as both an indictment and an invocation? How can the wounds that the earth is suffering from be anything but intimately, inextricably connected to the suffering of people?

II

The whole creation has been groaning.

—Romans 8:22

Every year on Ash Wednesday, which marks the start of the Lenten season, many Christians receive the imposition of ashes. This usually involves a priest or pastor making the sign of the cross on the forehead with ashes and reciting words from Genesis 3:19: remember "you are dust, and to dust you shall return"

(NRSV). These somber words invite us to reflect on the frailties of life, on the uncertain duration of our time on earth, and on the inevitability of our mortality. Ash Wednesday is a solemn reminder that death is the great equalizer. It comes for the rich and the poor, the high and the low, the foolish and the wise.

But we don't pay enough attention to the actual dust, this substance from which we emerge and to which we will return. The fact that we are created from the very raw materials of this earth, and that we will one day return to that material, should compel us to treat the spaces upon which we tread with great care, love, and respect. Our physical and spiritual health, even our very existence, is deeply connected with this planet on which we live and move and have our being. How we treat the soil matters. How we treat the air and water matters. How we treat our mountains and our rivers matters. We can be faithful caretakers and stewards of the very dust from which we emerge, or we can be destroyers of it.

For people of faith, environmental justice is a theological position. And environmental justice must be racial justice, which is God's justice for all God's people. These acts of justice are intertwined and cannot be separated. How we treat the land and how we treat those who work the land are intimately tied. There can be no true love of God's creation without a love of all those who occupy that creation. When one population bears a disproportionate share of the negative consequences of how we treat the environment, it is a sin against God's command to love one another. Where we dump toxic waste, when we fail to advocate for clean water, when we allow mountaintop removal and fracking—all speak to the groaning of the whole of creation. These are the death pains of a world where exploitation of both people and the environment triumphs over the faithful stewardship to which we have been called.

This exploitation of the natural world happens when people mistake domination for stewardship. As stewards or caretakers, we as the people of God are to lovingly tend to the earth; as Genesis 2:15 commands, we are to "cultivate and care for it" (NABRE). Domination is any practice whereby natural resources and human resources are exploited and abused without a care for renewability, sustainability, or righteousness. Too many treat the earth and the soil the way they treat other human beings: as disposable and expendable.

Ash Wednesday's mournful reminder—that we are dust and that to dust we will return—should focus our attention not just on death but on life. How do we live, fully and with integrity, between our beginning and our certain end? How are we called to spend the time between the dust of birth and the dust of death? How will we treat all the elements, all the people, of a world entrusted to us? And what spiritual and material inheritance will we leave for our children and their children?

The answers to these questions must speak to personal and corporate responsibility for our environment. God so lovingly cared for this world that God gave breath to human beings created from the dust of the ground (Genesis 2) and the stardust of this universe. For scientists now tell us that "every atom of oxygen in our lungs, of carbon in our muscles, of calcium in our bones, of iron in our blood—was created inside a star before Earth was born."

That we are made from dust and stardust—emerging from a soil so ancient that the dinosaurs may have tread upon it, connected to a cosmos so vast that it is beyond our comprehension—fills me with awe. How can I help but marvel at a single drop of water, which has changed forms multiple times through the water cycle over billions of years and yet can still quench my thirst?

May we emulate the Divine by breathing life into dusty, neglected, abandoned, and abused spaces and people. May we reject the human impulse to conquer and colonize and embrace the sacred task of being caretakers.

III

Neither the one who plants nor the one who waters is anything, but only God, who makes things grow.

—1 CORINTHIANS 3:7

As a daughter of the Black church, I was immersed in the stories, metaphors, and parables of the agrarian people described in the biblical text. This language of soil and seeds and crops was a part of my vocabulary as a child, even though I had never seen a farm or a field or more dirt than what was contained in the pot of a houseplant until a group of cousins and I were shipped to spend the summers in the rural South. In Sunday school and Bible study, I learned all about good seeds and good soil, bad seeds and poor soil. The language of reaping, sowing, and harvesting was church talk, and it blended seamlessly into the vocabulary of a church kid being reared on the stories in the Bible. More than anything, the message of John 15 was figuratively planted into my spirit: that good trees bear much fruit.

And because I wasn't just being raised in the church but in a capitalist nation, in my mind *much fruit* quickly became synonymous with success. And success became synonymous with numbers. Very early I learned that the way you could gauge if someone was a "good tree" was by the *amount* of fruit produced. It took me a long time to learn that the quest for quantity as a measure of success was simply a recipe for exhaustion.

Both my chosen fields, higher education and ministry, use numbers as a means of evaluating success. Like many colleges and universities, my alma mater sends her alumni a yearly boast of the record number of applicants for admission, along with the tiny number of admits. These numbers supposedly tell us something about the success of this college, how desirable it is that tens of thousands of high schoolers apply. Spots at the most coveted colleges and universities are a bit like the lottery: many will play but few will win.

The church world isn't much different. One time at a church leadership seminar, I heard a speaker boast of growing his small church from two hundred members to over two thousand. This required a new building and additional worship services. They had to create a parking lot ministry to handle the traffic and parking.

In both these cases, people pay good money to sit in rooms to hear how institutions and their leaders achieve "success," as evidenced by the numbers of all this great fruit they are bearing. Yet in both cases, the statistics actually tell you very little. While fifty thousand people may apply for a particular college, it is probably only the right place for a very few of them. A handful of colleges may top every ranking list, but that doesn't mean any one of them is the place where any given student will thrive. While two thousand people may have their names on the roll at a church, that number says absolutely nothing about whether lives have been transformed, bodies have been healed, or souls have been saved.

A school is not successful because of a large number of applications. Its success must be measured by its quality of teaching, its cultivation of the desire to learn, its joy and delight in asking hard questions and searching for meaning. A church is not successful just because it has a packed parking lot. Are believers becoming genuine disciples? Is the pastor an actual shepherd to the flock? Is the church serving as a hospital for the sick, or is it only a social club for the healthy?

I had to shift my thinking away from *much* fruit as a measure of success to the transformative qualities of *healthy* and *life-sustaining* fruit. Scripture never explicitly says what I now understand: that there's a lot of rotten, unhealthy fruit out there. *Just because it is plentiful doesn't make it good.* Just because the numbers are big doesn't mean the product is better. And just because the auditoriums or sanctuaries are packed doesn't mean the message is any more godly.

I struggle with this daily, living in a world that places so much value on numbers like salary and other quantitative markers of success. I try not to fall into the trap of measuring my own success by the numbers, but I often do. More money and material wealth, more people reading my books or attending my classes, more shouts of "Amen" while I'm preaching: these things would make me feel more successful, I think. Many of us want the tangible trappings of success that come along with "more." But like a tree that is growing into maturity, I am learning that not only do those tangible trappings tell you very little; the quest for them often leaves you drained and depleted. Trying to keep up with the Joneses, or at least the curated social media version of them, is impossible.

It took me a long time to realize that trying to achieve arbitrary standards, which were not created with me in mind, was leaving me exhausted. I kept trying to succeed in places that weren't built for me. I kept measuring my worthiness in institutions that were created explicitly to exclude me. I believed that my value was in my labor. I was taught that if I worked really hard and if I worked all the time, then the outcome of plentiful fruit was certain. But my reality kept failing to match this expectation. At times I've worked extremely hard, given a project all I've had, and still failed. At other times my paltry efforts were rewarded beyond my comprehension.

We often expect a one-to-one correlation between our labor and our fruit. And when it all seems arbitrary, we feel ready to give up. How dare our hard work and faithfulness not be rewarded? Why should we keep laboring in the vineyard while those sitting on the sidelines reap more rewards? Where is the fruit to show for our years of obedience and sacrifice? Where is all the stuff— the bigger house, nicer car, vacations? Why is no one inviting us to Martha's Vineyard? And why do we have to pay for our own Beyoncé tickets?

These are theological questions, pressing ones, for those of us who have been taught that the laborer was worth her reward, that these were the earthly markers of the fruit our obedience would bear. As a Black person in America, I have been taught that I had to be twice as good and work twice as hard to even be considered half as good as my white counterparts. I was taught that only an overabundance of accomplishments can counter the reality of racism. I had to have advanced academic degrees to do what someone else didn't need a single degree to do. I had to write more articles, mentor more students, teach more classes, and take on more responsibilities to prove that I was a team player and to refute the racist stereotypes of laziness and inferiority. I had to work more, smile more, forgive more, try more, suffer more. And so I did.

One day, God not so quietly whispered to my soul: my undue focus on much fruit instead of good fruit, my undue focus on material success and fear of failure, was preventing me from focusing on the True Vine. My eyes were on the prize instead of the process. I began to realize that God never demands that I work myself into a state of exhaustion and barrenness to meet an arbitrary standard the world has set. Depleted people, like depleted soil, produce *no* fruit at all.

The parable Jesus tells in Matthew 13 began to make sense: the farmer sowed good seed, but sometimes the ground was inhospitable or rocky. Sometimes the soil had eroded and was shallow. Sometimes birds ate the seed. That's just the way nature works, and it may seem arbitrary to us. Yet, when the conditions are right, the soil will serve its purpose and bring forth good fruit. You need good soil, healthy seeds, fresh water, life-giving sunshine, and much patience to bear good fruit. And while this cultivation process requires that the farmer do her work, it is God who ultimately brings the increase.

In his *Disciplines of the Spirit*, theologian Howard Thurman reminds his reader that the farmer is not in control of the outcome of his planting and sowing. "There are many forces over which the individual can exercise no control whatsoever," he writes. "A farmer plants a seed in the ground and the seed sprouts and grows. The weather, the wind, the elements the farmer cannot control. The result is never a sure thing. So what does the farmer do? He plants. Always he plants. Again and again he works at it—in confidence and assurance that . . . seeds do grow and they do come to fruition."

I'm trying to reorient my definition of success to being a planter of seeds, a good farmer. I'm trying to focus more on the planting, cultivating, and tender, loving care of my work, and less on the increase I can expect. Can we define real success not in the numerical yield of the fruit produced but in our simple obedience to the God of the harvest? Whether financial success or awards or accolades ever come, I am still called to tend the soil to which I've been entrusted. I am called to keep planting, again and again. But I am never, ever called to exhaust myself in the process. I am more than my labor, more than whatever rewards may or may not come through that labor.

I also believe that the same recipe that is healing the wounds of my own insecurities can heal the wounds that have been inflicted on creation: Handle with gentleness and kindness. Rebuke the demons of overwork and exploitation. Allow time for rest and recovery. And remain confident that the True Vine has grace sufficient for every need.

I am trying to stop measuring my success by other people's metrics and be gentle with my own spirit. I am resisting the impulse to work until my body collapses just to counter negative racial stereotypes. I am acknowledging that I cannot serve others from an empty cup and that I need regular rest and renewal. And I am leaning confidently on God's strength and not my own to do the work my soul must have. Womanist theologian Katie Cannon often used the phrase "doing the work the soul must have" as a plaintive reminder of two important questions that can help us resist the exhausting impulse of overwork: "Whose standards am I following? Are they intended for my flourishing or harm?"

Leviticus 25 admonishes us that the land needs a Sabbath's rest and a time for renewal, just like people do. And just like a fresh layer of snow gives the ground a chance to heal and returns necessary nutrients to the soil, a gentle and tender stewardship of creation allows for a bountiful and sustaining return. Domination, colonization, and exploitation may yield a temporary harvest, but they do so at far too great a cost to people and to land.

God can enrich and restore even the most depleted of soil. God can heal land soaked in ancestral blood. If the trees of the field will one day clap their hands, as the psalmist assures us, then God can take that which is parched and exhausted and bring forth new life.

TRUST BETRAYED
WOUNDED IN THE HOUSE OF A FRIEND

I

What are these wounds in thine hands? Then he shall answer,
Those with which I was wounded in the house of my friends.
—Zechariah 13:6 (KJV)

Over lunch, a white colleague wanted me to affirm his assessment of student behavior in the classroom. It was a well-worn version of the "young people today" rant familiar to many teachers and professors: *students don't read the syllabus; students are afraid to challenge the readings; students don't speak up in class.* I'm sure teachers at every grade level lament the same set of grievances.

On that particular day, however, I didn't want to play along. Thus my colleague was shocked (shocked!) when I told him that his experience in the classroom did not reflect my own. How students responded to him, what they said on his evaluations, even their choice to always use his honorific title and not his first name: these are all connected to the realities of race, class, and gender, I said. Identity markers matter in the classroom setting, I told him, and my experience as a professor diverged a great deal from his.

I've had to correct students who assumed they could call me by my first name instead of "Professor." I've had to deal with students who thought I was incapable of selecting the proper readings and wanted to correct my syllabus with their choices. I've been the one at the head of the class while a student has disrespectfully spoken over me and challenged my decades of research and experience. And as an administrator, I've read the teaching evaluations for women and people of color where students critiqued in detail the outfits they wore or their style of speaking.

My colleague quickly dismissed my statements, including my argument that faculty who are women and people of color have radically different experiences in higher education than our white male counterparts do. Despite the decades of research that confirm this, despite the books and journal articles written about this, my colleague simply could not believe—*did not want to believe*—that a different power dynamic exists when *I* enter the classroom than when he does.

Something important appeared to be at stake for him in this belief that our experiences were the same. On the most benign level, he was seeking solidarity with a colleague over the kind of trivial things professors complain about all the time. On a more serious level, he was invested in a false, colorblind, post-racial narrative of the world, in which things like race and racism no longer matter and certainly don't interfere with the intellectual work being done on a university campus. Yet here I was, a colleague he respected, arguing from both my own experience and decades of peer-reviewed research that the landscape of higher education was not the egalitarian ideal he needed it to be. I was disrupting his assumption that being in the same place equaled experiencing the same circumstances. We shared a campus but lived in different worlds.

This conversation was remarkably similar to one I had years earlier, when I had first arrived at this same bucolic college town. My hosts at a dinner party had waxed eloquent, for an extended time, about how this was the best place in the world to raise children, how this location offered the best quality of life in the entire country. My hosts and other guests explicitly stated and implied, again and again, how "lucky" I was to work and live in such an ideal setting—as if somehow random chance had brought me to this place and not decades of work and sacrifice.

I have learned to be silent in these situations or to nod agreeably. It is the wisdom of time that reminds me to choose which racial battles to fight. And yet, something important is being suggested by these seemingly trivial conversations—something that goes far beyond the small talk available in those settings. In this case, the cities and towns that regularly make the "Best Places in America to Raise a Family" list, to which my hosts referred in their conversation over dinner, only consider one idealized kind of family, which does not reflect my family. My dinner hosts and I lived in the same town, but in two separate versions of it.

So many questions went unasked at that dinner. Is a town a "best place" when you have to drive an hour to find someone who knows and understands the texture of your hair? Is it a "best place" when your brown-skinned daughter is the only one providing the much-lauded "diversity" at the elementary school? Is it a "best place" when, despite owning your home, people regularly view your presence in "their" neighborhood with suspicion and trepidation? These best places in America are deliberately homogeneous, with just a dollop of racial or ethnic or economic diversity: they're just diverse enough that they won't be accused of being unwelcoming to "minorities," but not enough to change the structures, priorities, or systems. Just diverse enough that residents can proclaim there's good "ethnic" food in the area but not so much that there is a critical mass of ethnic *people*.

In a world where whiteness is normative, white people don't have to think about the challenges an individual Black person or Black family may experience, which shape our perceptions of a place. In fact, to even speak of those radically different experiences is to be labeled "ungrateful." That was the common denominator in those two separate conversations: how fortunate I was to work at this school or live in this town, and how anything less than uncritical enthusiasm was somehow a marker of my ingratitude. And let me be clear: the expectation was not a posture of gratitude toward a gracious and loving God, who blesses us exceedingly and abundantly, above which we can even ask or imagine. If *that's* the type of gratitude we're talking about, I'm here for it. Rather, many white people want the performance of gratitude to human gatekeepers for their supposed benevolence toward the undeserving.

Black folks are often told, implicitly or explicitly, "You should be grateful." When Black students complain about racism on elite college campuses, someone always offers that they should be grateful they've even been given the opportunity, presumably having "stolen" a place from a more qualified candidate who would keep quiet in the face of hostility. When a Black homeowner complains about being profiled in his own neighborhood, he should be grateful to even live in such a nice place, where people are performing surveillance in order to keep out the "wrong" kinds of people. When a Black female executive complains that she is being underpaid in comparison to her peers, she's told she's lucky to even have the job; I mean, think of the hordes of other women who *wouldn't* complain, who would just feel thankful.

Black Americans are taught that casual racism and micro-aggressions are simply the cost of the American dream, that a spirit of gratitude is expected even for the wounds the American dream inflicts. When offered crumbs, we should be grateful to the ones brushing them away from their bountiful tables.

But it is exceedingly difficult work to love the place that wounds you. America, while a beloved home, has deeply wounded so many of those who have loved and defended her best. In contemporary culture, we use the term *wounded warrior* to refer to active-duty military members or veterans who need mental or physical assistance when they complete a tour of duty or end their military service. But with my historian's lens, when I hear of wounded warriors, I think, too, of the million-plus African American veterans who served during World War II and of the deep psychological and spiritual wounds they endured.

After honorably risking their lives in a war on foreign soil, they returned home to the contradictory messages of "thank you for your service" and "due to racism, we won't be able to thank you for your service." I often wonder how they were able to continue to love a nation that failed to love them in return. Black and white veterans shared a country but lived in different worlds.

Thousands of Black veterans who managed to leave the theaters of World War II in Europe alive were accosted, assaulted, and attacked upon their return to the United States. An untold number were lynched. Langston Hughes captures some of these contradictions in his 1943 poem "Beaumont to Detroit," in which he writes about the fact that Black people were excluded from the very notion of democracy for which America was supposedly fighting. The country had "jim crowed" Black people *before* World War II, he wrote:

> *And you're STILL jim crowing me*
> *Right now, this very hour.*

The GI Bill was a sweeping set of benefits first instituted for returning World War II veterans. The GI Bill is often credited with creating the American middle class as we know it, giving ordinary men and women the chance to access the American dream of higher education and home ownership. It helped millions to achieve a level of material comfort previously unknown to all but the richest members of our nation. Among the benefits were programs to provide college tuition, low-interest home loans, and unemployment insurance to returning veterans, many of whom were tragically young when they went into battle. For those who survived, the GI Bill was a program both to reward veterans and to provide them with the means for social mobility. Given the great sacrifices veterans had made on the nation's behalf, the GI Bill seemed like the least the nation could do. Many still view it as an incredibly successful government program.

But instead of a program administered by the federal government as initially proposed, one Mississippi congressman successfully fought for it to be administered by individual states—with devastating impact. Given the unchecked authority of states to make unilateral decisions about its implementation, the GI Bill was turned into one more lever of white supremacy. It became one more way that states allowed the spirit of Jim Crow laws to legitimize anti-Black racism.

The 1.2 million Black veterans who were entitled to the benefits of the GI Bill because of their heroic service were systematically denied those benefits at the hands of individual states. Some Black veterans could not access benefits because they were never given paperwork indicating their military service or any honorable discharge. Some Black veterans who qualified for benefits could not find any desegregated facilities, like vocational training programs, which could deliver on the bill's promise to provide veterans with employable skills. Since Veterans Affairs did not actually administer loans, when Black veterans tried to access their promised low-interest mortgages, they discovered that their in-state, white-run financial institutions could—and did—refuse to give them loans. Even if they could somehow secure loans, many returning Black veterans encountered restrictive housing covenants, which prevented them from purchasing homes in qualifying neighborhoods. When qualified Black veterans attempted to make good on promised college tuition, segregated colleges and universities simply denied them admission.

The GI Bill had neither the provision nor the power to dismantle centuries of systemic racism, Jim Crow, segregation, or disenfranchisement. One statistic concerning the GI Bill encapsulates the entire problem: a survey of thirteen Mississippi cities found that in 1947, African Americans received only two of the 3,229 home, business, and farm loans administered by Veterans Affairs.

Eighty years and three generations later, I am left to reflect on the ongoing wounds the systematic denial of GI benefits to Black World War II veterans has wrought. All I need to do is consider the poverty and financial insecurity that has haunted my own family. How many generations of wealth-building capacity have been lost because my grandfather, a veteran, was left empty-handed after returning from a war he did not even want to fight? What if he, the child of share-croppers, had been able to access the GI Bill and complete his education instead of trying to carve out a living without even a high school diploma? What if he had been given the means to secure a mortgage loan, instead of spending decades in segregated public housing, never to know the feeling of land he owned beneath his feet? What if an integrated vocational program had been available to him after his service? Would that have spared him from a lifetime of physical labor in low-wage, backbreaking jobs? What if home ownership, which we know to be the primary driver for economic security and wealth accumulation in this nation, had been available to him instead of the inflated rents and substandard housing of redlined urban enclaves?

The answer is this: it would have changed everything. Had my grandfather reaped the benefits of his service, as his white comrades did, he may have completed his education, gotten a mortgage, and been able to save for the future. Instead, as a member of a dispossessed group, my grandfather had a radically different experience of citizenship than the privileged in the same nation.

Eighty years later, I carry the weight of being the first generation of my family to crawl out of poverty. I am the first generation to be college educated. The first generation to own property. I carry the expectations and the burden of trying to pull everyone else out of poverty with my one salary, and I feel overwhelmed at how to undo the damage of the generational curse of American racism. My heart aches with the knowledge that I am three generations behind, and I find myself desperately trying to redeem the time for the generations ahead of me.

In blessed memory of my grandfather, I wonder what it means to be wounded in "the house of my friends," as Zechariah writes. I wonder what it was like for him to be wounded in the house of a nation: the only place you have to call home, but where you wonder if a "me" is included in this celebrated democracy.

II

When he rose from prayer and went back to the disciples, he found them asleep, exhausted from sorrow. "Why are you sleeping?" he asked them. "Get up and pray so that you will not fall into temptation."

—LUKE 22:45–46

Womanist theology asks questions of the Bible to expand the breadth and depth of possible scriptural interpretation. The text is still speaking to believers, as different generations, different readers, different peoples, and different cultures engage the ancient words of the Bible. Even after two thousand years, sermons and commentaries can offer something fresh and relevant to stories that have been told and passed down through many lifetimes. This wide sweep of interpretive possibility is particularly true of something as well-known as the passion narrative: that final period leading up to and including Jesus's crucifixion.

Christians place a heavy significance on the physical suffering Jesus experienced on the cross. Our art, our hymns, and our sermons emphasize and even glorify the crown of thorns placed on Jesus's head, the spear that pierced his side, the nails driven into his hands and feet, the sweat that was like drops of blood, and the bloody stripes endured on our behalf. The passion of Christ, his physical suffering, reminds us of the *humanity* of Jesus, who suffered under these horrific conditions as any other human being would suffer, and of the *divinity* of Christ, who is able to supernaturally atone for our sins and ultimately defeat death.

In a world where physical violence is ubiquitous, we become comfortable imagining the violence of the cross and centering our theology on it. Blockbuster Hollywood movies have spared no expense in depicting the excruciating details of the violence that takes place at the cross. In some churches, by centering the violence of the cross, suffering *itself* becomes a sacred act. People are told that if they suffer more, if they experience even more pain and more violence, they can more closely connect with Jesus's actions. An abused woman might be counseled to return to her abusive partner with the adage that she is suffering like Christ suffered. In too many of our religious spaces, suffering is made to be the sacred act on the cross instead of the loving work of redemption and the defeat of death.

My theological question is: How should we talk about Jesus's suffering *prior* to the cross? And why? Before the nails, before the thorns, before the lash, and before the dying: What was Jesus experiencing and why does it matter? And what do we learn about Christ when we consider the pain he endured *on the way* to the cross?

Jesus experiences some wounds that did not leave a physical mark. The Gospel of Luke describes Jesus praying at the Mount of Olives, hours before his death, knowing that his human sojourn is about to come to a violent end. When he returns to his friends, he finds them asleep.

According to Luke, Jesus's friends are "exhausted from sorrow." We might call what they are feeling anticipatory grief; they know their teacher is about to die, and they are already grieving this immense loss. Jesus wakes them up with a rebuke: "What business do you have sleeping?"

The Gospels of Matthew and Mark record that Jesus chastises his friends upon finding them asleep, saying: "Weren't you able to keep watch with me for an hour?" Mark records that Jesus wakes up his disciples three separate times. Returning the third time, he said to them, "Are you still sleeping and resting? Enough! The hour has come" (Mark 14:41). Christian tradition maintains that not just any disciples accompany Jesus during these final hours of life; he chooses Peter, James, and John to watch and pray with him. Yet in his hour of greatest need, even his inner circle, his closest friends and confidants, fall asleep.

Yes, the disciples were probably exhausted. Yes, the disciples were probably grieving. But I think about Jesus, fully human, with the foreknowledge of his impending crucifixion, struggling with the pain and loneliness of realizing that the ones closest to him failed when he needed them most. At this point in the passion narrative, Jesus has already prayed words of genuine vulnerability, asking his Father, if possible, to take this cup—this heavy weight of needing to atone for the sins of the world—from him. Knowing that his request was impossible and that he alone could fulfill this holy assignment, Jesus returns to his friends and finds them asleep. While he had been praying, in agony and anguish, his friends were sleeping. Instead of helping to pray him through his pain, the disciples succumbed to their own physical needs.

All four of the Gospels record this moment of loneliness, allowing us to speculate about the myriad emotions Jesus may have experienced when friends and loved ones fail. Disappointment. Betrayal. Loss. Abandonment.

We, too, experience wounds that forever transform us even if they never leave a tangible trace. This interior suffering: it matters. The wounds that are inflicted before anyone even touches Jesus: they matter. Even when it fails to leave a scar, our pain—particularly the harm done by those whom we love and trust and who claim to love us—is real. Well before Jesus arrives to his destiny at the old rugged cross, many friends and loved ones have already abandoned him. He is cursed and blasphemed, with all manner of insults thrown at him. He is mocked and reviled, accused of crimes of which he is innocent. He is betrayed with a kiss from a friend he loved. He is denied three times by the very person he trusted to build the foundation of his church.

Is there a betrayal that pains deeper than having your trust violated? Is there a wound that hurts more than being betrayed by someone you love? While most of us will thankfully never know the type of physical suffering Jesus endured, almost all of us will experience this interior agony.

The intimacy of personal betrayal is a heavy burden to bear, and there are few remedies to heal the lifetime of pain it causes. What do you do when friends fail? When family members abandon you? How do you heal when the rapist is a friend, when the betrayer is a sister, or when the violator is a parent? Where do you go when an intimate partner is the purveyor of violence instead of being your safe haven and rock? Or as the verse in Zechariah prompts us to ask: *What happens when you are wounded in the house of a friend?*

If the church has been the site of your abuse, can you ever return? If your family has been the source of your condemnation, where can you go? If your friend has been the one to mock you and revile you, can you ever trust her? If your lover has betrayed you, can you ever open your heart to love again?

Traditional Christian theology places all the emphasis for the redemptive work of Christ on the blood that was shed on the cross. But the biblical text spends most of its hermeneutical power detailing what happens *before* and *on the way* to that sacred event. Maybe that is where we can locate divine possibilities for living and loving again, even when we've been so deeply wounded in places and by people in whom we've placed our trust.

With divine foreknowledge, Jesus knew the events that would lead up to his death. He knew the human propensity to sin and to harm. He knew that imperfect people love imperfectly. In his final moments, he loved. And he rebuked. He comforted. And he chastised. He pleaded. And he surrendered. Before and on the way to the cross, we see the full range of Jesus's humanity, the mirror to our own. And that rich complexity is all we have to bring to the fraught situations in our own lives.

It is a risk to love again when one has been hurt. We need grace and tenderness for those who do the math, run the calculations, and decide that they can't take that risk again. May we provide the soft cushions they need to pack away their hearts until, or if, they ever decide to love again.

It is a risk to trust again when one has been betrayed. We need empathy and understanding to support those willing to reenter the fray, those who choose to step back into the building or work to forgive their trespassers. May we dig into the wellspring of our own imaginations and believe that a new way forward is possible.

It is a risk to return to a place where one has been wounded, with no guarantee or certainty that the same harm won't happen again. But it is also a risk to never return, to never open ourselves up to the transformative power of redemption and change. May we find the courage to admit that only hindsight brings perfect clarity on the decisions we have made.

Because if we are honest, we have been both the betrayed and the betrayer, the afflicted and the perpetrator. We've been both the recipient of harm and the one who has harmed others. I have been the sleepy friend in the garden, having the best of intentions but failing to step up when I've been most needed. And I have been the person denied and betrayed, left to pick up the shattered pieces of trust and my sense of self-worth.

We want the biblical text to give clear-cut answers to all of life's hard questions, and it does not. Life is much like the Via Dolorosa, the difficult and sorrowful path of Christ on the way to the cross. We stumble and fall. We get back up and try again. We encounter love and we suffer loss. Sometimes others, like Simon of Cyrene, help us to bear our burden. Other times the burdens are ours alone to bear.

My grandfather never said one word about his military service or the injustice of having received no GI benefits to his own children or grandchildren. We've only discovered and pieced together information long after his death. As his descendant, I am left with more questions than answers. The thought that life could have turned out radically differently for our entire lineage gnaws at me. As I remember everything from the unquestioned precision and exacting discipline that governed our household to the financial vulnerability that was always lurking around the corner, I am left to grapple with old information in a new light. While I don't recall seeing any scars on my grandfather, the wounds were there nevertheless.

Whether we are wounded in the house of a friend or in the nation we call home, my prayer is that we can begin the complicated process of healing. We can acknowledge that even when we occupy the same space, time, and events as others, radically different outcomes may be the result. And it only because of God's tender mercy, God's unfailing compassions, that we are not consumed with despair and hopelessness.

INNOCENCE IS THE CRIME

THE WOUNDS OF INHOSPITABLE PLACES

I

You will see that no prophet is to arise from Galilee.
—John 7:52 (NRSV)

Native New Yorkers are a cynical lot. In a city that never sleeps, we feel like we've seen it all, and nothing surprises us or catches us off guard. A naked man playing the guitar in the middle of Times Square? We greet him with a shrug. A-list celebrities walking through Soho, a blockbuster movie being filmed in the park? Not a second glance, just a sigh for the inconvenience. Seeing a Fortune 500 CEO or billionaire tycoon on the crowded subway? So commonplace as to be unremarkable. Living in a popular tourist destination, New Yorkers avoid tourists—and the places they visit—at all costs.

I carry this cynicism with me when I travel, so I was in full skeptical mode the first trip I made to "the Holy Land." A pilgrimage to the places where Jesus was born, ministered, and died: it's a trip many Christians dream of taking. Yet I struggled with the tourist traps we encountered there. Everyone tries to convince you that *this* spot is where Jesus walked. Maybe he did. Or *here* is where a particular miracle happened. Maybe it was. Tour guides want you to believe that *this* is where some important, amazing thing in the Bible took place. Maybe.

I didn't need well-meaning tour guides to understand I was standing on holy ground. But I also knew that, like at other "holy" sites, many unholy things have happened—and keep happening—in this region. I knew enough of the complicated and contested political, economic, and religious developments in the region to know that nothing was as simple as tour guides would like it to be.

The first destination on my trip to Israel and Palestine was a completely different experience, however. It was a leisurely boat ride on the Sea of Galilee. This body of water is deeply significant to Christians. We believe that this is where Jesus walked on water and where Jesus spoke to the storm and the winds obeyed his command. We believe Jesus performed a miracle here—feeding thousands with a few loaves of bread and a few fish. We

INNOCENCE IS THE CRIME

believe that this is the location where Jesus gave his Sermon on the Mount and also where Jesus called some of his disciples to become "fishers of men," rather than just fishermen (Matthew 4:19). On a beautiful spring day, as the boat slowly explored the beauty of this waterway, I was reminded of two things I never gave much attention to before. First is that the Sea of Galilee is not a sea; it is a lake. And second is that people are still fishing in her waters.

The Sea of Galilee is a freshwater lake whose currents are primarily driven by wind and whose water is supplied solely by streams, rivers, and rain. With a boat equipped with an engine, it's easy to travel the entire distance of the lake, which is about the same size as Washington, DC. It had taken me hours, on a plane doing five hundred miles per hour, to cross an entire ocean. When you are on that plane for hours, watching the tracker slowly make its way across the Atlantic, you get a sense for how vast an ocean is in comparison to a small lake. But to ancient eyes, Galilee was a mighty sea, immense and difficult to traverse if you had to row its entirety in a boat with handmade wooden oars. It was dangerous to sail if the wind and rain created large waves and unsafe conditions.

And commercial and recreational fishers continue to work the Sea of Galilee today. They deal with the same atmospheric conditions described in the biblical text. On my visit, I was greeted by small boats and large boats, hauling in their catch of fish for the day, people eking out a living from the small variety of fish found in this lake. We ate at a local restaurant that served fish pulled from the water that very day. I marveled at the fact that despite cycles of droughts, low water levels, overfishing, and other environmental concerns, fishermen and fisherwomen were still working on the shores of Galilee, using many techniques that were thousands of years old. I pondered if the people I met fishing were the descendants of those called by Jesus so long ago. Were they connected to the lineages of Peter, Andrew, James, and John, those whom Jesus promised to make "fishers of men?"

Christian believers ascribe huge theological significance to this small lake. Our hearts proclaim that Jesus, the incarnated God, did important things at this place. But grappling with the literal smallness of the place—that it is a small lake in a small town and not a mighty, raging sea—doesn't at all diminish the power it represents. Rather, it helps us understand a God who calls people from the lowliest of circumstances. Our prophets and griots and chroniclers often emerge from places that others would dismiss.

At the end of John 7, the Pharisees attempt to insult Nicodemus by suggesting that he is from Galilee, just like Jesus. "Surely you are not also from Galilee, are you?" they asked him. The religious authorities considered the people from Galilee rural and ignorant. The ultimate insult the Pharisees could give was to suggest that "no prophet" would ever emerge from the backwaters of this rural town by the lake, which was home to Jesus and his ragtag group of followers.

What happens when the broken and wounded are willing and able to tell the truth in a way that the healed and whole cannot? When poet and rapper Tupac Shakur asks, "Did you hear about the rose that grew from a crack in the concrete?" he is echoing the question posed in the Gospels about whether anything good can emerge from discarded and dismissed places. Can a prophet come from Galilee? Can anything good come from Nazareth? Can a person or a people with scratches and marks, bruises and lacerations, carry strength we should marvel at rather than overlook? What terrible, holy truth might someone who has survived the inhospitable places of life speak?

This small lake in the middle of a small country becomes the site for momentous events that have shaped the development of Christendom. A lake fished by humble people in the most humble of surroundings—not a palace or a royal court, the center of a metropolis or a grand university—was the site of perhaps the greatest sermon in human history. With its themes of love, forgiveness, justice, and human equality, the Sermon on the Mount, and the beatitudes contained within it, poetically summarizes the teachings of a poor carpenter's son, the child of an unwed mother, someone who spent most of his time with thieves, prostitutes, tax collectors, and the disreputable.

For my generation, the poetic words of rap artists like Tupac Shakur, DMX, and Jay-Z offer prophetic wisdom that comes from marginalized people who survive the inhospitable places and circumstances into which they were born. In his poem "The Rose That Grew from Concrete," Tupac Shakur brings together the image of a rose, a natural creation of great beauty, with concrete, a hard and unyielding substance. And he challenges our preconceptions about both. The rose can be scratched, marked up, and bruised, while the concrete can actually be fertile and fruitful.

Likewise, God turns the world upside down by giving us a savior from the margins, a messiah born a pauper instead of a prince. In doing so, our faith must take seriously the lessons taught by those too often neglected or silenced.

II

One might have hoped that, by this hour, the very sight of chains on black flesh, or the very sight of chains, would be so intolerable a sight for the American people, and so unbearable a memory, that they would themselves spontaneously rise up and strike off the manacles. But no, they appear to glory in their chains; now, more than ever, they appear to measure their safety in chains and corpses.

—JAMES BALDWIN, *THE CROSS OF REDEMPTION*

On display at the Smithsonian National Museum of African American History and Culture is a tiny pair of wrought iron shackles, restraints so small that the shackles could only have been used on an enslaved child.

During my time working at the museum, I would sometimes go and stand before these impossibly small chains. Before the museum opened for the day and the deluge of visitors arrived, I'd walk from my office to the exhibit and stand before the glass case that held these tiny shackles, almost paralyzed by their meaning. This display case is on the bottom level of the museum, surrounded by other artifacts from slavery, including pieces of a ship. The lights are deliberately kept very low to evoke the horror of the Middle Passage journey.

These shackles measured only 2.5 inches in diameter. Whether on slave ships or at the auction block, young Black children were chained. They were torn from their families, sold like furniture, and confined to slavery for life.

These shackles are centuries old. Yet as I stood there, I could not fail to reflect on the current world, which still targets Black children for extrajudicial punishment via the cradle to prison pipeline. Yes, some of these contemporary chains are metaphorical. But other chains are real. Tangible. Literal.

Take, for instance, the shackling of pregnant inmates and prisoners even when they are in labor. In most states of our nation, it is legal to use handcuffs, leg shackles, and belly chains on pregnant, laboring, and postpartum inmates. Women of childbearing age, particularly Black and Brown women, are among the fastest growing segment of the incarcerated population, increasing at nearly double the rate of men since 1985. The use of chains, shackles, and other restraints restricts a woman's ability to walk and move freely during labor and to assume various birthing positions. It increases the risk of falls and injuries to the pregnant person and the fetus. And it makes it more difficult for healthcare providers to treat their patients, who are confined to jails, prisons, and detention centers. Shackling during the postpartum period, then, can hinder a woman's ability to recover fully and to hold or feed her newborn.

The utter cruelty of it all is the point. The prison sentence is the official, court-ordered punishment for any crime that has been committed. The shackles, and other types of forced confinements, are the unofficial sanction. They are an excess, an affront to inmates' dignity and humanity, and a reminder of who wields authority and can dole out punishment.

As I stand before these horrors—the historical use of shackles on enslaved children, the contemporary use of restraints on incarcerated pregnant women—I am left to grapple with whether anything good can ever emerge from these sites of pain and trauma. What positive and life-giving things can possibly grow from the unyielding concrete of racism, fear, and exploitation?

We are a nation, James Baldwin suggests, that wants to measure our safety and our righteousness by the numbers of corpses and people in chains. It's as if we believe that handcuffing kindergarten-aged children and confining those in labor are actually procedures that can keep us safe from danger. An unending appetite for punishment, bloodlust, and chastening of the most vulnerable makes its way among us. Meanwhile, the evil deeds of the powerful and privileged go unchecked.

This culture of cruelty greets me every morning when I read the news. My heart hears echoes of the refrain of those crying out for Jesus to be crucified despite the fact that he never committed a crime. "But they cried, saying, Crucify him, crucify him. And he said unto them the third time, Why, what evil hath he done? I have found no cause of death in him: I will therefore chastise him, and let him go. And they were instant with loud voices, requiring that he might be crucified" (Luke 23:21–23 KJV).

This happens each time that we literally or metaphorically shout "kill them" or "lock them up" when confronted with the poor, the uninsured, the imprisoned, and the least of these. Rather than working to create national policies that improve the lives of all people, we offer up the lives of the impoverished, the unemployed, the underemployed, the unhoused, and many others as evidence of their moral defects. And we do not acknowledge our own unpunished moral failings or precarious circumstances. The cries to remove, to incarcerate, to punish, and to erase are the loudest when directed at those outside our small circles. It is easy to chastise those outside of our insular group, the select group we deem worthy of second and third chances. Meanwhile, we believe, the Other should be immediately put under lock and key and forgotten.

We build private prisons at breakneck speed while elementary schools fall in disrepair. We jail children and teens by the thousands, while we cut funding for afterschool programs and school lunches. We seek neither to prevent nor to rehabilitate those caught in the throes of our (in)justice system. We cry for our elected officials to chain these criminals and throw away the key, or to chain them and then kill them. Our bloodlust insists that if we chain them and kill them, then we will be safe. Yet we fail to direct that same cry for punishment toward those who commit corporate fraud, insider trading, embezzlement, or money laundering. Such "white collar crimes," according to sociologist Edwin Sutherland, are "committed by a person of respectability and high social status."

Here is what we rarely admit: We desperately want to remove the crimes of the impoverished and disenfranchised from our sight because of our *own* vulnerability and shame. We are ashamed to face the fact that many of us are only a paycheck away from being uninsured or facing homelessness or facing tough choices for how to survive. And we fervently want to identify with those of wealth and high status, wishing that we had the financial means to shield us from the consequences of our sins and bad decisions.

We are living in a delusion. We will not be a safer nation because we allow state-sanctioned murders via the death penalty. We will not be made safer by a multibillion dollar prison industrial complex. We will not be a safer nation because we routinely stop and frisk Black and Brown people without just cause. We certainly will not be a safer nation because we prosecute the ten-dollar theft and leave the million-dollar theft untouched.

In our bloodlust for more chains and corpses, we have created a nation that is all the more cruel, more prejudiced, and more unconscionable. Worshippers may sing the song "Break Every Chain" on a Sunday and then, on Tuesday, vote for officials who explicitly promise more chains, more incarceration, and more peonage, particularly for Black and Brown bodies.

As Christians, we claim we want to be more like Jesus. But the truth is that far too many of us would have joined those jeering and mocking him, ultimately calling for his death. There were far more people in the crowd shouting "crucify him" than there were those who wanted to spare Jesus's life. Seeing how quickly and violently the crowd turned on Jesus, most of us would have joined the death chants, lest the crowd quickly turn on us, too. We are not nearly as brave or heroic as we imagine ourselves to be. Most Christians have a lot in common with the thief on the cross, who, despite being in the same circumstance as Jesus—his own execution imminent—still joined the crowds and reviled and cursed Jesus.

How do we move beyond our human desire to identify solely with the innocent and crucified Jesus? How do we admit that our innocence is a myth we construct to hide our sins and our flaws?

III

> *It is the innocence which constitutes the crime.*
> —James Baldwin, *The Fire Next Time*

It is easier to imagine that we are the persecuted than the persecutor. It is easier to imagine that we are the injured party than the person holding the knife.

If you believe yourself to be, like Christ, lowly, meek, and mild, then you fail to see yourself as the executioner, carrying out the death penalty. Because that is the truth of our human condition: a willful forgetting of the harm we have done so that we can plead innocent to the crimes for which we are guilty. Writer James Baldwin condemns this posture of innocence, particularly white innocence, which he describes as white people's willful ignorance of racial realities: the deliberate forgetting of this country's history, the calculated amnesia. The crimes committed are bad enough, but for the authors of such devastation to declare their innocence— *"I didn't know"*—is also a crime.

This denial of responsibility is how we are socialized in a racist country. Through the whitewashing of history, the genocide of Indigenous persons and the enslavement of African peoples can be obscured, replaced by a false memory of how this nation was born. Innocence allows an individual today to attend institutions enslaved persons built with their hands, to hold weddings at plantations where families were forcibly torn apart, and to enjoy the rising stock prices of companies whose wealth was built on the slave trade. It allows you to proclaim, "I have nothing to do with that crime that happened so long ago," even as your portfolio continues to reap the financial dividends of these crimes. Every single person living in the United States, whether a newly arrived immigrant or a descendant of the Mayflower, is a beneficiary of the system of chattel slavery that built the physical and financial infrastructure of this country. We continue to benefit from the labor of enslaved people, and our denial of those benefits doesn't make the fact any less true.

Perhaps the example of the penitent thief on the cross next to Jesus can help us come to terms with our sins, both those we haven't acknowledged yet and the ones of which we are aware. According to Luke, as one of the criminals reviles Jesus, mocking his claims of being the Messiah, the other criminal rebukes him and says: "Have you no fear of God? . . . We have been condemned justly, for the sentence we received corresponds to our crimes, but this man [Jesus] has done nothing criminal" (Luke 23:40–41 NABRE). This same man asks Jesus to "remember me" when Jesus comes into his kingdom.

Here we have two thieves: one who has come to terms with his crimes and the reasons he is being punished, the other who spends his last moments mocking and reviling Jesus, failing to acknowledge his crimes or express any remorse. Between the two thieves is Jesus, innocent of the accusations against him and yet willing to sacrifice himself. If we open ourselves to this encounter between two criminals and Christ, we may find lessons for today.

The first lesson is that we need a fear of God—not in the sense of being afraid but in the sense of feeling awe and reverence. We stand in awe that God-in-flesh was present with the criminalized and the marginalized, and that this same God is still with us today, still present in the muck and the mire of our world. We often evoke the spirit of Immanuel, God-with-us, when retelling the nativity story of the birth of Jesus. But the theological concept of God-with-us encompasses more than the story of a baby born in a manger. God is ever present, ever with us, even at our lowest point. And while we may turn away from God, God never turns away from us. Even at the very hour of his death, Jesus turns his face *toward* sinners, both the one who is remorseful and the one who is unrepentant.

A second lesson we learn is that the penitent thief takes responsibility for his actions; he acknowledges that he deserves to be condemned for his crimes. There is no false cry of innocence, no denial of culpability. There is only an admission of his flaws. This penitent thief models the conditions under which forgiveness can take place by first naming what has been done and who has been harmed. When James Baldwin insists that it is the "innocence" that is the crime, he is reprimanding those who want forgiveness and racial reconciliation without truth-telling.

We learn a third lesson from this story in the final request of the remorseful thief. He asks to be remembered by Jesus when Jesus comes into his heavenly authority. Note that the thief doesn't ask to be forgiven. Maybe he believes he doesn't deserve forgiveness due to his crimes; maybe he doesn't know or believe that Jesus has the power and capacity to forgive him. He simply wants to be remembered, even in his imperfections and shortcomings. Even the least among us—those we've locked up—are remembered by God. We may choose to forget the ones we think are irredeemable, but God remembers and offers them mercy.

This penitent thief is the rose from the concrete of the ancient world: a convicted criminal whose crime was serious enough to have him executed. He is a confessed wrongdoer. While some versions of scripture translate his identity as a "thief," other possible definitions include "criminal," "evildoer," "bandit," and "gangster." You could say he was a "thug" of the ancient world.

And yet the text focuses not on the man's failings but on his faith: his ability to believe God and request that he be remembered after his imminent death. He is an imperfect man, leading an imperfect life, but he is saved by God's perfect grace and love, which cover a multitude of sins. And as Christian believers, we should find it extraordinary that God again and again chooses thieves, murderers, prostitutes, adulterers, and the like—and redeems them from the wages of sin and death.

God chooses a group of poor fishermen who can barely haul in a catch to feed their families to be leaders and apostles and architects of a faith. God chooses a criminal condemned to death to be remembered for his audacious faith. God chooses a poet-rapper, gangster, and self-described thug to remind us that something beautiful and delicate can be birthed from the most hostile of circumstances.

And so we cannot rest in a place of racial innocence. We cannot ignore the misdeeds and transgressions, the crimes and the violations, that birthed our nation into being. But we can marvel that from Galilee and Nazareth, from the South Side of Chicago and Compton, from concrete and asphalt, prophets and poets have been called. And from these inhospitable places, those willing to speak truth to power are still being called today.

8

THE RISEN ONE
UNTIL I TOUCH THE WOUNDS

I

Jesus said, "I took my stand in the midst of the world, and in flesh I appeared to them."

—GOSPEL OF THOMAS 28

You cannot read the stories of the resurrected Jesus as accounts of life triumphing over death without contending with layers of grief, mourning, and pain. A beloved mother has lost her first-born child; students and disciples are grieving the death of a teacher, confidant, and friend. Everyone has borne witness to the excruciating pain of the cross, the consequences of daring to defy empire, and the cost of declaring Jesus as Messiah. Some believers go into hiding, and others are confused about who they should now follow.

In the chaos of this time, the risen Savior shows up again, and again, and again—not as a ghostly, ethereal being but as wounded flesh. "Look at my hands and my feet," he says to some of the frightened folks to whom he appears. "It is I myself! Touch me and see; a ghost does not have flesh and bones, as you see I have" (Luke 24:39).

Only one of the four Gospels relates the extraordinary story of Thomas, a disciple of Jesus, and his reaction to the post-resurrection appearance. The other disciples tell Thomas that they have seen the risen Savior, but Thomas insists: "Except I shall see in his hands the print of the nails, and put my finger into the print of the nails, and thrust my hand into his side, I will not believe" (John 20:25 KJV). A week later, the disciples gather together again, and this time Thomas is with them. And although the doors to the room they are in are locked, the risen Savior once again appears. Knowing the doubts that Thomas expressed a week earlier, Jesus encourages Thomas to touch the wounds on his resurrected body.

This story earned him the moniker *Doubting Thomas*. Most Christian commentaries focus on Thomas's lack of faith—his inability or refusal to believe the word of his fellow disciples or even his own eyes. But I am less interested in Thomas's doubts than I am curious about the need, the pressing desire, to touch the physical body, the wounds, of Christ. I want to understand Thomas's longing to feel the wounds, to touch what has not yet had time to heal. I want to shift the ontological weight of the story away from Thomas's doubts and instead interrogate how, in this moment, he makes the physical body of Jesus a site for theological reflection.

How do we understand God-in-flesh, broken and vulnerable, and yet also resurrected and triumphant? How do we, like Thomas, make meaning of Jesus with his still visible wounds?

To Thomas, Jesus speaks the words, "Put your finger here; see my hands. Reach out your hand and put it into my side" (John 20:27). There is no parallel to this in the many other appearances the risen Savior makes after the crucifixion. Scholars believe that Jesus appeared to more than five hundred people during these forty days between his resurrection and ascension, but we are aware of no other time that he invited someone to put their hand in his side.

There is an intimacy to Jesus's command to Thomas, a closeness that we cannot overlook. Christ invites him to touch the unhealed wounds—to feel the places where nails and spear had pierced his body. It is a proclamation that the physical body still matters. Even after Jesus had defeated death, he appears to the disciples as a man with wounds. Lest there be any doubt in his humanity, Jesus makes it clear: he has experienced the fullness of human suffering unto death, and that kind of suffering leaves you marked and changed. Wounds, too, are a part of the divine story.

Because Thomas is not with the disciples during the first visit Jesus makes after the resurrection, another week passes before he is able to touch the wounds of Jesus. That means this encounter occurs at least ten days or even two weeks after the crucifixion. What if, in God's infinite wisdom, Thomas's request to touch and feel the wounds is to not only assuage his doubts but also to acknowledge the profound fact that healing takes time? If even the wounds of the risen Christ do not immediately close, why do we expect our own wounds to heal in such a hurry?

This is a theology for the wounded, for those who are still healing, and even for those who aren't quite ready for healing. The risen Savior insistently welcomes the doubting, the uncertain, and the grieving to touch and see that he is real and present and here with us. The risen Savior, who had been abandoned, denied, betrayed, and crucified, doesn't hide his wounds or rush their healing. As wounded people encased in the frailties of human flesh, can we, too, summon enough grace and kindness to acknowledge that our own very human wounds need time to heal?

After Jesus invites Thomas to touch him, Thomas responds, "My Lord and my God!" It is an affirmation that Thomas finally believes that this is his beloved Teacher. Jesus then replies: "Because you have seen me, you have believed; blessed are those who have not seen and yet have believed" (John 20:29).

Jesus never rebukes or condemns Thomas; he doesn't dismiss Thomas's request or offer a pithy parable in response to it. Just as he had done at the cross, Jesus presents his very body as the sacrifice—and this time, he presents it to a single person who needed physical evidence.

Were the wounds still tender? Did Jesus risk re-traumatizing wounds that had begun to heal? On this the scripture is silent. We are simply left with the accounts of approximately ten or twelve occasions, over the course of forty days, in which Jesus appears after the resurrection, in the flesh.

This is an embodied theology. In these stories, the physical body and the tangible world are consistently presented as ways of intimately knowing God. Some saw and believed; others have not seen and still believed. At the center of both experiences is God-in-flesh, loving us in our own wounded places.

II

Let us not rush to the language of healing before understanding the fullness of the injury and the depth of the wound.
        —LITANY FOR MICHAEL BROWN

I wrote a litany after the death of Michael Brown, an unarmed eighteen-year-old African American teenager who was shot and killed by a police officer in Ferguson, Missouri, in 2014. Michael

Brown's death, like many others before and since, sparked protests, marches, and direct actions aimed at holding law enforcement accountable for the seemingly never-ending brutality experienced by African Americans.

As I watched these events unfold, the unreasonable demand for forgiveness from those who have been harmed troubled my spirit. It still does. Black mothers, whose children had barely been buried, had microphones shoved in their faces as they were asked: "Do you forgive the person who murdered your child?" Before a trial, sometimes even before a funeral, a family member was called upon to forgive the person who callously took the life of someone they loved, regardless of whether the killer was even repentant.

Why is this level of supernatural forgiveness required of Black people? What additional harm is done by rushing to declare forgiveness or rushing to declare healing, even while the pain is still occurring? And why are such unreasonable demands made of grieving families and grieving communities—demands that don't depend on either the apology or the remorse of the perpetrator? Despite my academic training and Christian upbringing, I lacked a theological framework to answer a question that haunted me in the wake of so much violence and despair: What do we do when we aren't ready for healing? How do we live in the between time: after the damage has been done but before forgiveness or healing can occur?

I wrote this litany out of my pain but also my need for more precise language to express the terrible hypocrisy of asking the wounded to make a grievous situation better. I wrote this litany because I was weary of the mask I was constantly being asked to wear because of my faith. People wanted to hear *words* of forgiveness without considering the *work* that is necessary for forgiveness.

A Litany for Those Not Ready for Healing

Let us not rush to the language of healing before understanding
the fullness of the injury and the depth of the wound.
Let us not rush to offer a bandaid when the gaping wound
requires surgery and complete reconstruction.
Let us not offer false equivalencies, thereby diminishing the
particular pain being felt in a particular circumstance in a
particular historical moment.
Let us not speak of reconciliation without speaking of reparations
and restoration, or how we can repair the breach and how we can
restore the loss.
Let us not rush past the loss of this mother's child, this father's
child . . . someone's beloved son.
Let us not value property over people; let us not protect material
objects while human lives hang in the balance.
Let us not value a false peace over a righteous justice.

*Let us not be afraid to sit with the ugliness, the messiness, and the
pain that is life in community together.*
*Let us not offer clichés to the grieving, those whose hearts are
being torn asunder.*

Instead . . .

*Let us mourn Black and Brown men and women, those killed
extrajudicially every twenty-eight hours.*
*Let us lament the loss of a teenager, dead at the hands of a police
officer who described him as a demon.*
*Let us weep at a criminal justice system, which is neither blind
nor just.*
*Let us call for the mourning men and the wailing women, those
willing to rend their garments of privilege and ease, and sit in the
ashes of this nation's original sin.*
Let us be silent when we don't know what to say.
*Let us be humble and listen to the pain, rage, and grief pouring
from the lips of our neighbors and friends.*
*Let us decrease, so that our brothers and sisters who live on the
underside of history may increase.*
*Let us pray with our eyes open and our feet firmly planted on the
ground.*
*Let us listen to the shattering glass and let us smell the purifying
fires, for it is the language of the unheard.*

God, in your mercy . . .

Show me my own complicity in injustice.
Convict me for my indifference.
Forgive me when I have remained silent.
Equip me with a zeal for righteousness.
Never let me grow accustomed or acclimated to unrighteousness.

While I wrestled with these questions, the words of the Lord's Prayer echoed in my spirit. I remember the first time I heard the recitation of the Lord's Prayer in which the speaker and congregation prayed, "Forgive us our *debts* as we forgive our *debtors.*" I remember it so distinctly because those were not familiar words to my ear. The version I knew was this: "Forgive us our trespasses as we forgive those who trespass against us." I was taught this version of the prayer as a young girl, even before I could read, and the refrain, unwieldy though it may be, felt more natural in my mouth. I was shaped by the idea of trespass even before I understood its definition.

Now, as I watched racialized violence and brutality unfold around me, with concurrent demands for instant forgiveness and immediate healing, the words of the Lord's Prayer helped me to push back: against both the false piety being displayed by those asking the question and the unbearable task being asked of Black people.

Forgive us our trespasses as we forgive those who trespass against us: the first task on the path toward forgiveness is for each person to acknowledge the ways that he or she has willfully and deliberately sinned; it is to admit that we have ignored the spiritual NO TRESPASSING SIGNS and that our thoughts, words, or deeds have caused someone injury. Forgiveness is dependent on our acknowledgment of our sins, both those that are deliberate and those that are unintentional.

That was the missing piece in so many of these accounts of racist brutality and killings of unarmed people: any acknowledgment that a wrong had been committed. The headlines about these crimes often appear in the passive voice, as if to suggest that the victim had harmed himself. In describing incidents of police violence, editors and journalists frequently use terms like *officer-involved shooting*, *suspect struck by gunfire*, or *tear gas was deployed*. All fail to acknowledge *who* did the shooting, *who* deployed the tear gas, *who* did the harm.

Political scientist William Schneider calls this passive voice "past exonerative tense." Such language, he suggests, which deflects attention from who is at fault, absolves anyone of accountability, and clears the air of any tangible wrongdoing. Consider this 2021 account of a shooting released by the Los Angeles Police Department: "one of the officer's rounds penetrated a wall that was behind the suspect, beyond that wall was a dressing room. Officers search[ed] the dressing room and found a 14-year-old female victim who was struck by gunfire." Instead of saying that an officer shot and killed a child, the writer, by using the past exonerative tense, fails to name the wrong and fails to name the perpetrator.

Forgive us our trespasses as we forgive those who trespass against us: When someone has trespassed against you, they have crossed a line or a boundary, violating your space and your very being. When we are courageous enough to forgive those who trespass against us, it is only because the person who has done the harm names the infringement and the violation. Naming is the first act toward repentance, which is necessary for forgiveness. The perpetrator of violence must admit he has done something wrongful and egregious if he wants to be forgiven.

When someone uses language that is demeaning and degrading, the sin is not merely in the language they use; the trespass is the assault on human dignity. When someone commits an act of violence, the trespass is not just a physical event but an infringement on one's value and worth. To physically trespass on someone's property is to insist "I have a right to cross into your territory, at will and on my own terms." It is to insist on your own privilege and the other person's submission.

The word *trespass* is weighty with legal undertones: violation, infringement, encroachment, intrusion. There are consequences and penalties for trespassing but there is also the possibility of forgiveness and reconciliation if one is willing to work. Everyone wants to be forgiven, but few want to do the sacrificial work of repair. Lutheran pastor and theologian Dietrich Bonhoeffer once said: "Cheap grace is the grace we bestow on ourselves. Cheap grace is the preaching of forgiveness without requiring repentance."

Instead of shoving cameras into the faces of grieving mothers and placing additional burdens on them to demonstrate grace and forgiveness, we should turn our attention to the violators. We should train our gaze on them, and we should ask them to explicitly identify and name the harm they have done, to genuinely repent their actions, and to repair or restore that which has been violated. Only then is forgiveness even a possibility.

III

In this here place, we flesh; flesh that weeps, laughs; flesh that dances on bare feet in grass. Love it. Love it hard. Yonder they do not love your flesh.

—Toni Morrison

Science has tried to quantify and qualify love. We can measure cortisol levels, dopamine, and serotonin. We can try to formulate oxytocin or vasopressin. But we cannot create the right chemical mix that occurs in our bodies when we are loved and when we love others. Nor can we fully express love within the limits of human language.

When I contemplate the sacrificial love of Jesus, I am reminded of the words of physician Bernie Siegel in *Love, Medicine, and Miracles*. "I am convinced that unconditional love is the most powerful known stimulant of the immune system," Siegel writes. "If I told patients to raise their blood levels or immune globulins or killer T cells, no one would know how. But if I teach them to love themselves and others fully, the same changes happen automatically. The truth is, love heals . . . I do not claim love cures everything, but it can heal and in the process of healing cures occur also."

The unconditional love of Christ on the cross, and the unconditional love of the Christ who displays his wounds, requires action to be fully known. Unconditional love *does* something to us. It changes something; it mends. *Agape*, unconditional love, is active. In the biblical text, *agape* is often connected to another verb, another action word, as in the famous 1 Corinthians 13 text where *agape* love hopes, endures, believes, and rejoices.

When Jesus inquires of Peter on three separate times if Peter loves him (John 21), the exasperated Peter replies that since Jesus knows all things, he must know of Peter's love. After each inquiry, Jesus gives Peter an assignment: "feed my sheep." The height and depth of Jesus's love had been made plain to the disciples. This was the last of Jesus's post-resurrection appearances. For forty days, he walked among his followers, reassuring them that he was the Messiah and that he had defeated death. How were they to demonstrate their unconditional love for their Teacher and Savior? By taking care of the other followers of Christ; by providing both literal and figurative food for other believers. The command to love is always paired with action: If you love me, keep my commandments. If you love me, feed my sheep. And unlike most human transactions, where we do something merely for our own gain or reward, *agape* love is turned outward: *love others, feed others, bring good news to others.*

It is easy to love the person who looks like you, acts like you, and thinks like you. It is easy to love the person who shares your values, supports your causes, and affirms your beliefs. It is easy to love the family whose house burned down or whose baby was sick. It is so much harder to love the unrepentant drug addict; the smoker still taking drags of a cigarette between puffs of oxygen; the thief robbing for the sheer adrenaline rush; or the person who thinks being cruel to others makes them a strong leader.

Perhaps this is why the story of Thomas and Jesus truly matters. If we are to love Jesus, we have to love the man with the still-healing wounds and not just the conquering hero. We have to love the broken Jesus and not just the triumphant one. Likewise, we have to love wounded people and wounded places. To work for flourishing and liberation in a broken world, we cannot look away from crucified flesh or be repulsed by the wounds. Instead, as Toni Morrison suggests, "in this here place," we must love the flesh and "love it hard."

In her novel *Beloved*, Morrison gives us an eschatological vision of a beloved community. She depicts a place of worship away from the surveillance of whiteness. In that place, the enslaved and the formerly enslaved can celebrate and mourn; they can dance and lament. Morrison creates this outdoor clearing where the Black body is not synonymous with auction blocks and bills of sale.

This community exists despite the larger world being a place that does not love Black people's flesh; a place that despises Black people and wants to see them broken. Through the words of Baby Suggs, Morrison reminds us to love our hands, love our necks, love our inside parts, and to especially love our hearts.

This is the holy lesson for those not ready for healing, for those who insist that they need to touch the wounds before believing: *healing takes time*. Broken people and broken places can be mended, but it may not happen immediately and it cannot be rushed. And *healing requires love*: unconditional love both for ourselves and for those the world finds hard to love. Love does not cure everything, but it surely heals.

TONGUES OF FIRE

9

THE HEART'S LANGUAGE AND WOUNDED BREATH

I

For anyone who speaks in a tongue does not speak to people but to God. Indeed, no one understands them; they utter mysteries by the Spirit.

—1 CORINTHIANS 14:2

I speak Black Church. That is my mother tongue. It is the language I learned at the foot of my grandmother, church mothers, and elders. It is the language I learned in the storefront church of my youth. I speak Black Church in my private devotions with God and when I am among the saints. I speak Black Church, the language of my ancestors, as a theological language centered on the justice of God.

When I learned in college that Black English, also known as African American Vernacular English, was a language, I wasn't surprised. Encountering the scholarship of Dr. Geneva Smitherman in her classic *Talkin and Testifyin: The Language of Black America* confirmed what I had always known: Black children are raised bilingual. They are taught to code-switch between the language they speak at home and the language they must use in public discourse. There is a distinct grammar, vocabulary, and structure to Black English that can be parsed and studied like any other language. It is neither "broken English" nor "slang," but rather a distinctive dialect with a history, origin story, and construction.

As a womanist theologian, then, I posit that Black Church is a specific linguistic category of Black English: that is, *Black Church is a language.* The hymns, parables, wisdom expressions, and biblical narratives have combined with Black speech to create a distinctive mother tongue for those who grow up in the Black church. All aspects of this speech are theologically inflected. For example, these are the lyrics of a spiritual that we often sing and that I find myself constantly referencing to this day:

> *I've got shoes, you've got shoes,*
> *All of God's children got shoes.*
> *When I get to heaven, goin' to put on my shoes,*
> *Goin' to walk all over God's heaven. Heaven, heaven.*

Ev'rybody talking 'bout heaven ain't going there.
Heaven, heaven.
Goin' walk all over God's heaven.

The verses of the spiritual are repetitive, with only the word *shoes* changing to other objects: crown, robe, harp, wings. For the enslaved who penned the song, having an actual pair of shoes was not at all a given. So to declare that one has shoes, or a crown, or a robe: this was to speak that which was not into existence.

And while being outfitted in heavenly garments may have been an eschatological hope, the lyrics also speak to divine justice. By insisting that everybody talking about heaven wasn't going to make it there, the song roots itself in God's judgment of self-righteousness. Some people, despite their holy talk and religious language, were not actually going to make it to heaven. They would be judged and found lacking, unable to enter the kingdom of God. Reflecting the belief of the enslaved in a God who turns the natural world upside down, the ones who lack shoes in this world—both the poor and the poor in spirit—will get to walk, fly, and shout all over God's heaven.

Such words, expressions, and songs helped me to develop an understanding of the Divine who is actively engaged in the lives of the faithful: a God who sits high and looks low. Language is the embodiment of experience, and the language of the

Black church taught me to be certain of the justice and goodness of God, in contrast to the injustice and cruelty of humanity. I had no trouble reconciling a God who is good all the time (and all the time, God is good) with the weight of human-generated harm and sin. And when we sang "none but the righteous shall see God," as one of verses of "Wade in the Water" says, I knew that the meaning was less about my own personal righteousness than the surety that a God of justice sees the deeds of the unrighteous.

To speak Black Church is to say "in that great gettin' up morning" as casually as someone else would say "have a good day." It is to laugh when someone compares something that is taking too long to a choir's "grand march." To speak Black Church is to understand what "Usher Board Number #2" is, or what it means to call someone "casket sharp." To speak Black Church is to dwell in a world of metaphors, similes, analogies, and linguistic wordplay all centered on a God who is present, active, real, and engaged in the lives of Black people. It is to believe in a God who never requires that we speak someone else's language in order to be loved and valued.

To affirm that Black Church is an actual language is not to deny that the Black church is also an institution: a fixture of Black communities, built by people of African descent, with historical specificity and material reality. In the United States, the Black church emerges as a response to enslavement and as a powerful indictment of white Christian nationalism. The Black church shelters fugitives, feeds the hungry, educates generations, and continues to stand as a site of affirmation, celebration, ritual, worship, and political agency.

But even if I were to leave the physical and historical space of the Black church, I could never abandon the words of my mouth and the meditation of my heart. You don't suddenly forget your language when you leave your country. You hold it close, and you speak it sometimes, even if just to yourself.

Some people dismiss sentences like "I've been 'buked and I've been scorned, I've been talked about sho's you' born" as the dialect of the uneducated and ignorant. But it is a part of my mother tongue, my heart's language, and I hear in those words the lament of a people who have faced oppressive systems, forces, powers, and principalities. I hear the language of a people who have been called everything but "children of God"—and yet who refuse to lay their 'ligion down.

II

In whose hand is the soul of every living thing, and the breath of all.

—Job 12:10 (KJV)

In the middle of the COVID-19 pandemic, people who were sick with the virus were encouraged to use fingertip pulse oximeters to measure their oxygen levels, with lower levels being one indication of the severity of viral infection. These medical devices had been designed and calibrated on either all-white or mostly white research subjects, and there was a significant skin color bias in the results. This fact had been known for decades and discussed widely in medical literature, but manufacturers, knowing of this racialized flaw, still failed to correct the design for products that people were now using at home to determine the severity of their illness.

For people with darker skin tones, pulse oximeters overestimated the degree of oxygen saturation, inflating numbers that were then used to make medical decisions. When Black patients reported significant trouble breathing, flawed oximeters often showed a "normal" result. Medical professionals then routinely disbelieved the patients, accusing them of exaggerating their symptoms, denying life-saving medical treatment, and even discharging them from the hospital. Patient care was based on a racially biased machine—again, a bias that has been known for decades and yet was still embedded in the device and the healthcare system.

The medical system in the United States has a long and painful history of undertreating Black patients. Medical school students are still regularly and erroneously taught that Black people have a higher threshold for pain because they have greater muscle mass or skin that is thicker than white skin. Sickle cell patients, the vast majority of whom are African American, are routinely denied pain medication when they are in medical crisis because of the unsubstantiated perception that many Black patients are drug-seekers instead of human beings in excruciating pain.

Imagine gasping for air, struggling to breathe, and being told that because this scientific device says that you're fine, you must have an adequate supply of oxygen. Imagine the cry of the urban asthma patient, living in a community where air pollution and toxic waste sends her to the emergency room crying "I can't breathe." And she is not believed or treated. Imagine being restrained in a chokehold and repeating eleven separate times "I can't breathe," while a video captures your last gasps. Imagine being handcuffed and detained, with a knee to your neck and back for nine minutes and twenty-nine seconds, crying "I can't breathe" and calling for your dead mother as the life drains from your body.

These are the wounds of racism, which are both systematic and personal. Systems like healthcare or criminal justice or schools are structures, and the bias within them is pervasive and deeply entrenched. A country's laws, written and unwritten policies, and long-standing traditions can perpetuate systemic racism. Where one lives or if one can vote or what school one can attend are some of the consequences and repercussions of these big systems. But systems don't exist in a vacuum. People, with their biases, flaws, and sins, make up institutions and structures and systems. Systems, just like individuals, can damage people and communities.

I wrestled with this information about pulse oximeters as it came to light during the pandemic. Like many others, I was cloistered at home and living in fear of the virus. My worry wasn't simply contracting the virus but that I would not be treated aggressively enough to survive it. If I got so ill that I had to go to the emergency room, would I be seen as someone in need of care, or would my distress be dismissed? I had the privilege of being young, healthy, educated, and of having a lot of friends who are medical professionals I could contact with questions. I had the safety net of a job with benefits, including excellent health insurance. I was well-equipped to advocate for myself and my extended family. But my heart grieved for the elders in my community who did not have an advocate at home; who couldn't access and download PDFs of the latest medical literature; and whose well-being was being ignored by a chorus of dismissals because of their age or other health conditions. I worried for those the system would not hear, those whose cries and pains would be ignored because of their race, weight, income, gender, or inability to convey their physical distress.

I can speak medical jargon, if needed, having learned as a Black woman to be extremely proactive in my own healthcare.

Research skills are the bedrock of any advanced degree program, and I arm myself with research when I engage the healthcare system. Or the legal system. Or any of the institutions and structures that I encounter.

But what about those who don't speak these languages? Who don't know the exact phrase to convince a nurse or doctor that they are suffering? What about those who don't know the right words to say to a judge or a jury? Or those whose experiences with these systems have been so horrific that they are rendered silent? Are they being heard? Are their cries of not being able to breathe under the constraints of racist and unjust systems being heard? And are the rest of us listening?

III

A crowd came together in bewilderment, because each one heard their own language being spoken.

—Acts 2:6

Fifty days after Passover, while celebrating the Festival of Weeks, the disciples of Jesus are once again gathered in an upper room. Their friend and rabbi has been crucified, resurrected, and he has now ascended. They are finally coming to the realization that Jesus was indeed the Messiah who had been promised. In this space that is a mirror of the Last Supper—and some commentators believe this event took place in the very same room as that last meal—the remaining disciples gather and experience an event that Christians believe is the birth of the Christian church.

The Holy Spirit enters the room like a mighty, rushing wind, filling the place with the *ruach* of God: breath, wind, spirit. All who are present begin to speak in other languages—languages that are not their own native tongues. Tongues of fire alight on them, on all those in the upper room who dare to believe that Christ has been raised from the dead. Other pilgrims in Jerusalem, who were from every nation under heaven, are astonished to hear the message of Christ in their own languages. The disciple Peter gives a sermon affirming that Jesus of Nazareth was indeed the Messiah, and three thousand believe and are baptized.

The Pentecost narrative holds a special theological place for me, as a child of the Holiness-Pentecostal tradition, because of its emphasis on pneumatology, or the work of the Spirit. The Holy Spirit, which is far too often treated as an afterthought in discussions of the triune God, has a special role in establishing the church, as suggested by the Book of Acts. Like tongues of fire, the Holy Spirit is the flame that fans the embers of this new religious movement. The Holy Spirit breathes life and vitality into what was a small group of students mourning the death of their beloved teacher, which grows into a fellowship, which grows into a movement, which grows into a worldwide church of billions of believers.

This newly forming church, these followers of the Way, begin their fellowship with a meal at a physical table. They eat together. Although it is initially only the disciples of Jesus who gather, the table is metaphorically expanded and enlarged as thousands as men and women hear the message of the risen Christ, receive and believe Jesus's teachings and his promise of eternal life, and are baptized in the name of the Messiah.

After the resurrection, the table where thirteen men had convened becomes the *ecclesia*: the body of Christ, in which every nation under heaven and every language under the sun is present. The church is born from a multiplicity of identities. It is the ingathering of *all* flesh. The scripture Peter uses for the first sermon of this new house church comes from Joel, in which God promises to pour out God's spirit "upon all flesh," including daughters and sons, the old and the young.

The intimacy of this spiritual encounter is reinforced by the specificity of the language. New believers and new disciples are hearing this message of life and abundance in words they can understand; they hear the good news of the risen Christ in their vernacular, not in someone else's language. All could hear and all were welcome to participate in this emerging movement.

I think of my ancestors' linguistic and theological refusal to abandon their faith, even in the presence of wickedness. I think of their words of faith, their songs of holy resistance, dancing like the tongues of fire of the Holy Spirit. These words of radical inclusivity echo in a spiritual my ancestors composed. As a child, I heard Rev. James Cleveland sing it on the albums my grand-mother played:

> *Plenty good room, plenty good room,*
> *Plenty good room in my Father's kingdom.*
> *Plenty good room, plenty good room,*
> *Just choose your seat and sit down.*

I imagined the day of Pentecost as a spiritual table, like the kitchen table of my grandmother's house, with room for whoso-ever will. The kitchen table of my childhood expanded infinitely on Sundays and holidays and special occasions, when the normal place settings for a family of four grew to miraculously accom-modate twenty or thirty or forty guests. There was always room for one more person, always food for one more guest.

I could not imagine a scenario in which someone would be turned away from our table. I still can't. I cannot imagine a fam-ily member or stranger not being embraced and welcomed with an offering of biscuits or pound cake. It wasn't just that there was *room* at the table; there was love and joy and laughter. The meal was already prepared for you. All you had to do was choose your seat and sit down.

Now, truth be told, as kids, we were regularly bumped from the table for adults. If the knock at the door brought another grown-up for dinner, I knew I had to give up my usual weekday spot at the dining room table. Some Sundays, and all the holidays, we had enough kids for a separate kids' table. Sometimes even the kids would be moved from the children's table to make room for the overflow of family or neighbors or church members. On those days, eating Sunday dinner or a Thanksgiving meal on television trays in the living room, when the house was filled to the rafters with company and all the other tables were full, felt like a special treat. What we learned as children is knowledge I now treasure as an adult: God multiples whatever we freely offer, including food and hospitality.

The multiplication of food at my family's table was a paradox, as miracles often are. There is a generosity in poverty that confounds prevailing wisdom. Growing up, I did not know that we were poor. Everyone around us was similarly situated economically. The families in our neighborhood and at our church represented the invisible working poor: those who scrub floors and load trucks. The chair of the deacon board at church was the janitor at the elementary school. One of my favorite church mothers emptied bedpans until she could no longer walk the halls of the hospital. My own grandparents never completed high school and raised two generations of children on nothing but hope and pocket lint. And yet they managed to feed everybody who came to our door. The depth of their generosity, and the generosity of all those who raised me, is especially astonishing to me now that I am the one who has to buy groceries, cook food, and pay all the bills. The people who most know deprivation, scarcity, and lack are often the ones who will give most freely, most generously, and without expectation of receiving anything in return. To know that God is a Multiplier is to believe that the last shall one day be first.

So the story of Pentecost entails the radical inclusivity of a table where all are welcome to sit and eat. Pentecost is also about the breath of God, about restoring life to the wounded and broken. For the family and friends of Jesus, still mourning his death, the breath of God brings comfort: their Messiah is yet alive and is preparing an eternal place for them. To the weary pilgrims traveling to Jerusalem, the breath of God brings restoration: after travels through various lands and countries, they hear the good news of Jesus in their own mother tongue.

To the women whose gifts had been denied, the breath of God affirms their gifts of prophecy. Daughters are no longer commanded to be silent. To those whose dreams were deferred, the breath of God gives new vision and purpose. For if resurrection after death is possible, so, too, are our impossible dreams and far-reaching visions. In a world that steals the life-sustaining breath of far too many, the Holy Spirit is a fresh wind—a deep, cleansing, healing breath to those struggling to breathe. For all who believe, the Holy Spirit is a Divine Comforter in a profoundly discomforting world. "For the promise is unto you, and to your children, and to all that are afar off" (Acts 2:39).

To hear the gospel in your own language, in your mother tongue, as did the pilgrims in Jerusalem, is to know that God created difference and loves all of creation and the multiplicity of language, identity, race, ethnicity, and culture that make up creation. Acts 2 says that Jews and converts to Judaism, Egyptians and Romans, Arabs and Libyans, among many other groups, all heard "the wonders of God in [their] own tongues."

I can't help but reflect on this in our contemporary setting, how significant it is for life and death information to be communicated in ways we understand. What does it mean for the Spanish-speaking mother to talk about her sick child with a pediatrician in her own language? What does it mean for a first-generation Korean immigrant to find a church and hear prayers in the same language his grandmother used to pray? How significant is it for an eighty-year-old struggling with illness to have her treatment and care explained in ways that are compassionate and not patronizing? Language matters. It matters if we understand the language being spoken to us. And it matters whether the tone and tenor of the message are dignifying.

While so much of the emphasis in the story of Pentecost is put on the miraculous *speaking* of other languages by the disciples, the true gift of the Holy Spirit is how each of us can *hear* from God in the language of our hearts. God whispers lovingly in our ears, whether in Cantonese or English, Hindi or Arabic. God never requires that we strip any single piece of our unique identity in order to be in communion with God and the people of God.

This is the holy lesson: where the Spirit of the Lord is, there is liberty. Where the Spirit of the Lord is, you can breathe freely and easily. Where the Spirit of the Lord is, you can worship in your mother tongue without having to code-switch or translate for others. We know that God understands even our groans and wordless utterances. Where the Spirit of the Lord is, difference is joyfully celebrated and affirmed.

Where the Spirit of the Lord is, there is room at the table for whosoever will come. There is warmth for the weary, and love to enflame your hope. There's welcome for the wounded and comfort for those whose healing still lies far and away in the future. There's a radical inclusivity that doesn't require you to abandon your identity or your dialect or your mother tongue or your heart's language. At God's table, you can breathe easy, take your seat, and sit down.

JUST KEEP ON LIVING

10

THE WOUNDS OF DISCONNECTION

I

*And he came to Nazareth, where he had been brought up:
and, as was his custom, he went into the synagogue on the
sabbath day.*

—LUKE 4:16

My favorite part of the baby dedication ceremony happens when
the minister takes the child into his or her arms and walks the
baby around the congregation. I have seen every reaction imaginable on the part of the baby. Some sleep through the entire
ceremony, including the walk, unaware that they are being dedi-
cated to God. Some cry the minute their parents hand them over
and don't stop crying into they are back in their safe and loving

arms. I especially love the curious babies: the ones who fiddle with the pastor's lapel mic, or play with his beard, or grab and eat her necklace.

It was my joy to be the officiant at a baby dedication not long ago. The little one slept through all my carefully planned words, and I felt an indescribable joy holding her, walking her among the community gathered there and reluctantly returning her tiny sleeping body, clothed all in white, back to her parents. We were not in a church, and I am not a pastor. The baby was the first child of some of my former students, and we had gathered in their home for this lovely ritual.

As I talked to their friends and various members of their families, however, a theme emerged that weighs heavily on my spirit. Almost everyone there had been a member of a Christian church at some point in time, but most were currently in the process of deconstructing their faith. I was among a group of twentysomethings and thirtysomethings who no longer went to church. The vast majority of them had been raised in religious environments but were now figuring out where they belonged, what they believed, and what traditions they would hold or discard.

I am deeply familiar with this process, having torn away the legalism and narrowness that defined so much of my own early faith. So deconstruction itself doesn't disturb me. Deconstruction can be necessary and healthy. It's what comes—or doesn't come—after it.

The deconstruction of faith is akin to the tearing down of an old building. In some cases you need a wrecking ball so that you can completely demolish the structure and leave nothing standing. In other cases you need the discernment and finesse to remove certain parts, brick by brick, and then figure out which other parts simply need some renovation. But in either case, at some point, you are left standing in the massive pile of rubble, surrounded by the bits and pieces of something you once loved deeply, something no longer standing. And as hard as deconstruction itself is—all the tearing down and the leaving behind—not having somewhere to live, somewhere to belong, and somewhere to go for answers is harder still.

Post deconstruction, do you rebuild? Or do you simply walk away from the rubble, the fragments, and the ashes? Post deconstruction, how do you imagine community? How do you imagine ritual? Where do you go to bless the babies or bury the dead? Who will stand before a congregation and speaking loving words of blessing over your infant? Who will speak final words over your loved ones as they are lowered into the grave?

Faith deconstruction is often accompanied by physical and social disconnection from community, which can become its own kind of wound. How do you tend to the wounds of disconnection—the very real pain of feeling unmoored from a community, values, and belief systems? When deconstruction leads to disconnection, where do we turn for the rituals and rites that provide life with meaning?

Rituals matter. While faith is what we believe, the tangible things that we *do* help us make meaning. We have rituals for celebrating a birth and a marriage; rituals for memorializing the dead; rituals for graduation and milestone events. These rituals create a sense of community and belonging, which endure over time. My alma mater's rituals, which I participated in over the course of my college experience, bound me to an academic institution so effectively that I will not even wear the rival college's (more attractive) paraphernalia to this day.

The rituals that are connected to rites of passage are particularly meaningful: how we mark the transition from childhood to adulthood helps us to bridge the past, present, and future. When we offer confirmation classes to children in church, we are teaching them that they belong to a community of faith, that this community of faith is tied to ancient traditions, and that they are the future leaders of that faith. And while religious spaces aren't the only location of rituals and meaning-making, I wonder where we locate those important rituals in an increasingly secular culture. And I mourn that so many feel so disconnected from the church that they no longer feel it is a valid space in which to celebrate or to mourn.

Sacred scripture in the Christian tradition provides us with very little information about the early life of Jesus. But in the few glimpses we have of young Jesus, he is engaged in rituals. He's carrying out rituals connected to the practice of his faith, which would have been true of any devout Jewish person in his era. The book of Luke tells us that Jesus was circumcised on the eighth day, as was the custom (Luke 2:21); that Jesus was presented for purification and consecration at the temple and blessed by Simon, a devout elder, and by the prophet and widow Anna (Luke 2:22–28, Luke 2:38). Mary and Joseph observed the Festival of Passover, and scripture tells us that at the tender age of twelve, Jesus is not only with them observing this sacred day; he was both listening and teaching at the temple, eager to always be in his Father's house (Luke 2:49). And as was the custom, Jesus could usually be found in the synagogue on the Sabbath day.

In other words, even the Incarnate God in human flesh participated in meaning-making rituals. As Jesus grows from infancy to adolescence and ultimately to adulthood, he remains connected to a community of faith. From circumcision to baptism, these rites and rituals—things that are done with hands and feet and the whole physical body—are intertwined with theology.

What we believe and how we practice are not two separate realms. Ritual weds belief (our theology) to the body (what we do). So to ask the question "How will you bury your dead?" isn't merely to inquire about which funeral home will handle the services. It is to ask difficult questions about the end of life: How do I want to be remembered? Who will offer those final words of consolation to my family? Or when I am the griever: What do I do with this great wellspring of grief I feel in my lungs and kidneys? And even years later, when my beloveds' remains have returned to dust but my grief still feels fresh and interminable—what rituals, and what people, help to mark the passage of time?

If rituals develop from the heart's great need for connection, community, and meaning, where can we meet those needs if we are disconnected from institutions and congregations and sometimes even estranged from our families? Have we been so successful in dismantling the very entities that facilitate these rites and rituals that we are left tending to our own wounds and brokenness, without help from a caring community?

If we deconstruct our way out of traditional Christian belief, which can indeed be narrow, and if we disconnect from the church, which is indeed flawed: What then? Where do we connect, and what do we worship? And to whom will we go in the moment of our greatest need? Who will weep with us, and who will rejoice with us?

II

Turn to me and be gracious to me, for I am lonely and afflicted.
—PSALMS 25:16

Every Sunday in my childhood church, a dutiful usher would hand out paper bulletins, which contained the order of service, important announcements, and other administrative information about Sunday's service. For the kids of the church, these bulletins became coloring books, fans, paper airplanes, and the stationery we used to pass each other notes. Week after week, year after year, the old photocopier near the pastor's office churned out church programs, and we put them to good use.

If your church was fancy, you had color programs with the picture on the front corresponding to the liturgical calendar. In my mind's eye, I can still see the photographs on the bulletins of churches we sometimes visited: those chunky red candles of Advent, or the white lilies of Easter, sometimes with a corresponding scripture.

My own church wasn't fancy enough for the colorful bulletins, but one constant, steady feature of our black-and-white programs was the sick-and-shut-in list. The sick-and-shut-in list featured people—including names, full addresses, and telephone numbers—who were sick at home, hospitalized, or otherwise unable to make it to church. Today, this would constitute a violation of privacy and even an invitation to fraud. But for us it was more like a holy to-do list—a reminder to pray and act. At some point in the service, we'd always pray for the people on the list, along with recently bereaved families, whose names and information were also often listed. But the list represented more than prayer. Our elders, deacons, and church mothers would also make pastoral visits to the sick-and-shut-ins. They'd take them communion or groceries or cards that children made in Sunday school.

Some names had been on the sick-and-shut-in list my whole life, including people I never met who lived in nursing homes and senior housing. We were encouraged to send cards and notes, make phone calls or visit. I frequently accompanied my grandparents to hospitals and nursing homes, waiting as they prayed or sang a hymn at the bedside of someone I thought must have been as ancient as days. I was the designated carrier of homemade soups and breads, casseroles or baked dishes that, despite our family's own poverty, we frequently took to the seniors' building. Christmastime meant me carefully addressing the envelopes of cards to be sent to everyone on the sick-and-shut-in list, in addition to family and friends. With the carefully printed letters of an elementary school child, and later the fancy cursive of a high schooler, I'd address stacks and stacks of cards, complete with holiday stamps, to be sent to people I never saw in the pews of our church.

These seem like such small acts, but the message was clear to me even as a child. That sick-and-shut-in list meant that you were still connected to a body of believers, even if you could not physically be present. If you were on that list, it meant that once a week, someone was calling your name out loud, and an entire church was stretching forth their hands as the elders prayed for you. Being on that list meant that you had not been forgotten. Even if you had dementia and were living in a memory care facility, no longer able to remember this church or her people, we were still remembering you.

This small Black church in Brooklyn, New York, was teaching me that connection matters. Privacy and self-sufficiency and independence might serve you well when you're young and healthy and can take care of yourself. But when you're sick or elderly or shut-in or dying, connection matters, and it matters profoundly. There are days I long for the knowledge that someone, somewhere, is praying for me, that someone has me on their mind.

And when, inevitably, a member of that sick-and-shut-in list died, we were expected to attend their homegoing service. As a teenager, I once asked my grandparents, unwisely, why I had to attend the funeral of someone I had never met *yet again*. Someone else had died—someone I only knew because her name was on a church bulletin. There is not a teenager on the planet who wants to go to a funeral for an old person they have never met. I couldn't understand why my grandmother didn't see this.

With her usual cryptic answer, my grandmother responded: "Just keep on living."

Just keep on living . . . The premise of this Black expression, which I'd heard all my life, is simple: if God is gracious to allow you to live long enough, you will eventually understand the answers to some of the foolish questions you ask. And I can say that I've now lived long enough to comprehend why that sick-and-shut-in list was important, why I needed to attend those funerals, and why I needed the rites and rituals with which I was raised. The loneliness of life and the afflictions of daily living sometimes feel more overwhelming than a person can bear.

Just keep on living . . . and that phone call or a card, personal visit, or a homemade meal will feel like a lifeline. If you live long enough, you'll see that these ministries to the sick, the bro-kenhearted, and the downcast are more than time-consuming obligations. They're essential means of connection and care that we, too, will someday long to receive.

Just keep on living . . . and you will want someone to pray over your newborn. You'll long for someone to offer you the communion elements when you can't make it to church. You'll be looking for that pastor to come and bless your new house or accompany you to the funeral home or meet you at the oncol-ogy ward. You'll want the church mothers to anoint you with oil when all the powers and principalities of an evil world feel like they are conspiring against you. You'll want someone to call your name before heaven, to stand in the gap and be an intercessor when you can scarcely pray for yourself.

Just keep on living . . . and you may learn that making a
life in the rubble of the faith you have deconstructed becomes
increasingly hard. The wounds of disconnection may never
heal in the debris, and you may struggle all your life with the
tension between wanting a community to which to belong
but having dismantled so much that a return may not be
possible.

Where is the healing for the wounds that may never heal, for
the fissures and fractures that may never be repaired?

III

*Heal me, O Lord, and I shall be healed; save me, and I shall
be saved: for thou art my praise.*

—JEREMIAH 17:14 (KJV)

Wound care is both art and science. Healing is both miraculous
and mundane. The body has an amazing capacity for repair, even
when a wound is more serious than a skinned knee. Almost as
soon as you get a cut or surface wound, your body begins to heal
the injury. In a truly miraculous process, your white blood cells
immediately fight bacteria that can cause an infection. Your red
blood cells go to work, along with your platelets, to form a clot
over the wound, and later a protective scab. And in the most
mundane fashion, most wounds can and will heal without much

medical intervention—that is, when they are cleaned and steril-
ized, properly bandaged and left to rest.

But the body is often operating under less-than-ideal conditions. If you are already sick and your immune system is com-
promised, healing will take much more time. If wounds are not
attended to in a timely manner or if infection sets in, healing may
not even be possible. What seems like a simple cut may eventually turn into a much more extensive problem. On the other
hand, a wound that seems deep and almost impenetrable may
quickly heal with scarcely any sign of trauma. One of the keys in
healing is the condition of the body at the time of injury. If the
body is relatively healthy when injured, healing tends to happen
more quickly.

When public health researcher Dr. Arline Geronimus proposed what she calls the *weathering hypothesis*, she gave language
to a phenomenon that Black women have long known: that is,
that constant stress, racism, and poverty damages the body and
leads to serious health conditions. As she writes, stress "literally wears down your heart, your arteries, your neuroendocrine
systems . . . all your body systems so that in effect, you become
chronologically old at a young age."

While not denying the role of diet, genetics, or exercise,
researchers like Geronimus recognize that the body responds
to social forces. It is no exaggeration to say that racism kills.
Diabetes and hypertension and strokes are often the physical

manifestations of racial weathering, befalling people who experience marginalization, discrimination, and prejudice at the highest levels. And a body already traumatized by these forces often struggles to heal from what appear to be minor illnesses or injuries.

So as a womanist theologian, I am struggling with how to reconcile the idea that healing may not be possible with my genuine belief that God is able to heal. How do I affirm the promise in Psalm 147:3—of a God who "heals the brokenhearted and binds up their wounds"—while acknowledging a fallen and broken world that reinjures and re-traumatizes those who are already most vulnerable? And what if the words of this beloved hymn are true—that there are some sorrows *only* heaven can heal?

> *Come, ye disconsolate, where'er ye languish;*
> *Come to the mercy-seat, fervently kneel;*
> *Here bring your wounded hearts, here tell your anguish,*
> *Earth has no sorrow that heaven cannot heal.*

I love this hymn's reference to the "mercy seat" and its plaintive refrain that "earth has no sorrow that heaven cannot heal." And yet I wonder: Are there some wounds and sorrows that, no matter how much time passes, cannot be healed on earth and must wait until heaven? Are there walking wounded among us longing for heaven (and the sweet release of death) only because it feels like their wounds and sorrows will never be healed on this earth? If so, perhaps the "mercy seat" is critical for our earthly healing.

The mercy seat in the Hebrew Bible refers to the gold lid that was placed on the Ark of the Covenant, a sacred symbol of God's power dwelling among the people. In the New Testament, for Christians, the mercy seat is a symbol of Jesus's blood sacrifice for our sins. Thus the mercy seat becomes a sign of atonement, the price that Jesus paid to redeem us.

But as a daughter of the Black church, I know that the *mercy seat* refers, too, to a physical place where you meet God. The mercy seat, altar, or mourner's bench is a place of divine encounter. In some Christian traditions, it is a literal bench or kneeler; in others, it is simply the space cleared in front of the altar at church. In almost all iterations, it is a space at the very front of the church, usually in view of or right beneath the cross. Many of our worship spaces today resemble a television studio, complete with an audience instead of worshippers, but some churches have retained this sacred physical space.

At the mercy seat, people tarry to hear from God, to make requests known before God. It is a place where people pray for salvation or healing. They pray for deliverance from addiction or to break generational curses. They pray for broken hearts and empty wombs. At this space, people bring their burdens to God with hope and expectation that not only does God care but that God will deliver and save.

It was at such a place that I found myself one day, filled with doubt, disbelief, and the rubble of all I had deconstructed. There, plagued with burdens, health problems, and the weight of it all, I challenged God with the boldness of child. Only children can be so reckless and dauntless and still believe that their parents will love them. There my heart cried: *God, I still believe in you, but do you believe in me?*

The answer I received while kneeling at the front of this church helped me begin to heal: there is a difference between healing and curing. To be *cured* of disease, sickness, or sorrow is often what we are suggesting when we use the word *healing*. We want a cure: for the agent of destruction to be completely taken away and to be left without any disease. To cure an infection means that there is no longer a trace of it in your bloodstream. To be cured of a disease means that it has been utterly vanquished from your body. Each trace of sickness has disappeared.

And while God can and does cure, *healing* is a different matter. Healing means that the injury and the trauma remain present, but we learn to live in wholeness despite that fact. Healing means that the disease may still be in our bloodstream, but each day we feel stronger. Healing means that there are fewer days of pain this week than last week. Healing means that, while the wounds may still be there and they may still ache, a protective scab can form. Healing includes hard days and even painful days but also an assurance that trouble don't last always.

Healing is a way of living in the world, taking small steps toward wholeness and peace. Healing is affirming ourselves even when we fail. Healing is rebuking whatever forces make us feel unloved and unwanted. Healing is saying no when our plates are full. Healing is finding a space of joy and laughter even in grief. Healing is a decision to get up and try again. Healing is coming to the conclusion that God sees me, believes in me, and walks with me.

I cannot eliminate the reality of racial weathering and the physical toll it takes. I cannot undo whatever genetic determinants may be lurking in my cells. I cannot solve the crisis of the plastic particles in the water I drink or the pollutants in the air I breathe. I cannot singlehandedly strike a blow to the painful history of racism in this nation and the physical and mental effects so many suffer because of it. I cannot remove the police officer's knee from a young Black girl's neck. And I cannot reassure anyone that Jim Crow will not rear its ugly head again.

But because I know that healing and justice are companions, nurturing my own healing is doing justice work. Helping others toward their healing is doing justice work. Heaven may be the ultimate cure for our sorrows, wounds, and cares. But while we are on this earth, the ability to love ourselves, love each other, and do the work of justice is how we can work toward God's promise of healing. The idea isn't that our bodies will never get sick or that we will never be wounded in heart or spirit. But our capacity to care for one another, to care for all of God's creation, brings both healing and justice.

If we just keep on living, as my grandmother said, we may discover that wounds bear witness to something beyond themselves, to a healing that is yet to come. That the disconsolate, the wounded, and the broken have worth and dignity in God's sight. And that we can entrust our anguish to the healing mercy of a crucified God. *Just keep on living* is a heartfelt statement of witness: over the course of a lifetime, you'll be able to see the profound evidence of God's mercy and grace even in the face of suffering or loss. *Just keep on living* is at the center of the Christian faith: a reminder that trouble don't last always and God will never leave you or forsake you.

Technology has changed, and so have privacy standards, but I am grateful for the example of the sick-and-shut-in list of my childhood years. I love how those lines printed on a black-and-white church bulletin echoed the words of the spiritual "Hush, Hush, Somebody's Calling My Name." We were a congregation calling the names of those near and far, those known and unknown. And we prayed earnestly for their healing. And now I pray that in an era of deconstruction and disconnection, in an age when we've abandoned so many rituals and traditions, we still find a way to tend one another's wounds.

DANGEROUS MEMORIES
A CONCLUSION

I

The wall of Jerusalem is broken down, and its gates have been burned with fire.

—NEHEMIAH 1:3

Distressed at the desolate condition of Jerusalem, her broken walls and her burned gates, Nehemiah, a cupbearer to King Artaxerxes, orders the rebuilding of Jerusalem's walls. Under his direction, in the span of only fifty-two days, the walls and the gates are rebuilt. Nehemiah not only helps to rebuild in the midst of rubble and despair; the Second Book of Maccabees says that Nehemiah is the one who brings the holy fire for the altar of the temple back from where it has been hidden during exile, and that Nehemiah also founds a library to house holy scriptures:

"And these same things were set down in the memoirs and commentaries of Nehemias: and how he made a library, and gathered together out of the countries, the books both of the prophets, and of David, and the epistles of the kings. and concerning the holy gifts" (2 Maccabees 2:13).

Nehemiah is engaged in work that I call "prophetic retrieval." He rebuilds the walls and gates of the sacred city among the ruins of her destruction. He restores and rekindles the holy fire in the rebuilt temple after it has been hidden and forgotten by most. And he builds a library to remember important people and places, as well as the power of God's provision. His prophetic work is to retrieve the history of a people, including recovering the flame, which was a symbol of God's presence.

Nehemiah's righteous work has become a model for me as a Christian. Ideas about rebuilding and restoring and remembering are elements of my own theological work. I imagine myself engaged, alongside other scholars, in acts of prophetic retrieval for believers today. While I'm far from a cupbearer to a king, I want to be engaged in this special ministry of retrieval and restoration as Nehemiah embodies it.

And yet I lament that when I was growing up, I was taught more about Nehemiah and the other characters of scripture—with their specific cultural, ethnic, and religious contexts—than I was taught about the richness of my own contexts. Raised in a Christian home, I found the characters of the Bible rich and present in my imagination. Years of Sunday school, Bible study, and regular worship services helped me to identify with a group of people who existed thousands of years ago, who spoke languages I had never heard, and who lived under social and physical circumstances I would never experience. This, I was taught, was the power of sacred scripture: to speak across time and spaces so that a little Black girl in Brooklyn could read herself into the story.

But this easy acceptance came crashing down for me when I dared to articulate a question I had wondered about for years. How could the bloodline and genealogy of people I had never met—but was encouraged to read about and memorize—be more important than the bloodline and genealogy of my own family and community? I was taught about the twenty-seven generations (or forty-two, depending on which Gospel account you read) between Jesus and Adam. I had names and details about the royal lineage that tied Jesus to King David. I could tell you how Boaz was connected to Abraham.

I could not, however, offer any insight into my own family tree prior to enslavement or much thereafter. In ways deliberate and unintentional, I was taught that the history of my own community from 150 years ago was less important to my spiritual and psychological development than the five-thousand-year-old history of people a world away. Daniel in the lion's den and David slaying Goliath were taught to children as stories of courage and strength. Yet somehow my own forebears' courage and strength in the face of the lyncher's rope and the slaver's whip were scarcely mentioned in church. I learned about the acts of resistance and boldness by Jael in the Book of Judges and Vashti in the Book of Esther; and yet, how my own ancestors poisoned the food or broke the tools of their enslavers as acts of resistance and survival never made a Sunday liturgy.

I wrestled with why my community's stories didn't seem worth telling in religious spaces. Why were they not worth mining for their sacred value and divine presence? Why were Christians—we who have a divine imperative to remember— deliberately excluding the stories of Black life, both the mundane and the extraordinary? Why were these stories also missing in the national secular conversation about the making and building of America?

This was a deliberate forgetting, I learned. Catholic scholar and womanist theologian M. Shawn Copeland perhaps best describes it when she writes:

> *We conspire to not remember; we choose to forget.* We repress and erase; we edit and delete. The result is a peculiar and unsettling, even puerile, ignorance that seeks to pass as political innocence. Christian exercise of memory purports to be radically different: We pledge to remember, we are obliged to do so. We are marked with a sign that neither can be erased nor easily forgotten.

Whether during the Eucharist, Ash Wednesday, baptism, or prayer, Christians are marked, or mark ourselves, with the sign of the cross. We may wear a crucifix or cross necklace; we may decorate our houses or offices with symbols of Christ's sacrifice for us. We are obligated to periodically assemble ourselves to remind each other of the God we serve and of God's love for us. We have signs, symbols, rituals, and traditions of remembrance that mark us as followers of Christ.

As a sun-kissed daughter of the Divine, I am marked by ties to a fraught history this nation conspires to *not remember*. This is a nation that deliberately chooses to forget. As a womanist theologian, I believe that retrieval work *is* prophetic work, that it is necessary for repairing, rebuilding, and restoring. Moreover, prophetic retrieval is the recovery of dangerous memories.

II

That this may be a sign among you, that when your children ask their fathers in time to come, saying, What mean ye by these stones?

—Joshua 4:6 (KJV)

We often lose a sense of how dangerous life was for the first followers of Jesus and for the people in the movement that emerged after his death. In our comfort and privilege, we have a hard time grasping the subversive nature of the gospel, with its embedded belief in a Messiah who came to turn the world upside down, a Savior who came to dismantle systems, powers, and principalities. And the modern-day church has truly lost sight of the danger of memory and its power to counter official narratives and state-sanctioned histories.

Dangerous memories are those kept alive by a particular community, largely through oral tradition or art forms. Their narrative retelling of what they witnessed, what they experienced, how they struggled, and how they survived often runs counter to how—*and if*—their histories are recorded in some official capacity. For the marginalized, the minoritized, the oppressed, and the silenced, community memory is dangerous precisely because it contains the keys to resistance, agency, and hope.

It is especially dangerous to remember the wounds: to allow the wounds to be a witness to the past and also a warning about the future. Layers of sediment give us a history of the natural world. We can discern seasons of drought and flood, epochs of ice ages and global warming, by reading the marks that still remain after millions, even billions, of years. Personal and historical wounds, those that are tangible and those that are intangible, likewise bear witness to seasons of distress and grief, along with seasons of joy and thriving.

Black Americans bear the historical wounds of the massacres in Elaine, Arkansas; Tulsa, Oklahoma; Colfax, Louisiana; and

Rosewood, Florida. Our wounds are a witness to the continuing harm of *Dred Scott v. Sandford*; *Plessy v. Ferguson*; and *Cumming v. Richmond*. We are forever marked by the knowledge that we have not come as far as we think from the Jim and Jane Crow era, that this nation is still comfortable crucifying the Black body because the very color of its flesh is suspicious. We live with the residual trauma of a world in which institutions built to protect and serve often bully and belittle, and where marches and rallies, protests and petitions, seem too little and too late.

And this is why dangerous memories are important: they call your soul to "look back and wonder" how you got over. How you managed to thrive in a world in which you were never intended to survive. The subversive and the ingenious are connected. And so we remember the enslaved women who braided grains of rice into their hair in order to cultivate crops in secret. We remember the feeding of the multitudes with corn bread and pot liquor, that still-nourishing liquid that was left behind when all the food was gone. We remember the families who "stole learning" when death was the penalty for literacy. We remember the secret messages of resistance and revolution embedded in the spirituals and also in the homemade quilts. We remember the underground economies and the courageous churches that sent fugitives to freedom. We remember the legal challenges, the freedom rides, and the scholarships funded by humble fried chicken dinners in church basements.

Thousands of years ago, Nehemiah, cupbearer to the king, was bold enough to help restore that which had been destroyed. He worked to retrieve the memories of his people and codify them in sacred scripture. Surrounded by the rubble of his community's own deconstruction, he was called to rebuild and repair so that no one would fall into idol worship and forget the one true and living God.

This is my work as a womanist theologian and a person of faith: to bless my origins through the retrieval of dangerous memories and to breathe life into those stories so that we never forget. Perhaps this is your work too: to weave memory into the present. To remember the subversive, ingenious ways of your forebears and ancestors, including their subversive and ingenious faith, which you have inherited.

And when the next generation asks about these national wounds and personal scars, we—*both you and I*—can tell them that they are a witness to the strength of a people, evidence of the long and continuing quest for justice, and a testimony to God's healing power.

ACKNOWLEDGMENTS

With continuing gratitude for all the ways you show up for me: Ally, Myriam, Melissa, Meta, Maggie, and Frank. And for my teachers, who poured knowledge into me and who gave me language for the stories inside my heart, I am forever thankful.

NOTES

Introduction

3   *"if you are silent about your pain":* Irie Lynne Session, Kamilah Hall Sharp, and Jann Aldredge-Clanton, *The Gathering, A Womanist Church* (Eugene, OR: Wipf and Stock, 2020), 102.

6   *"drawing us all toward the goal":* Troy R. Saxby, *Pauli Murray: A Personal and Political Life* (Chapel Hill: University of North Carolina Press, 2020), 278.

Chapter 1

10   *This site is an incredibly disturbing one:* Kristina Killgrove, "Archaeologists Find Bound Bodies of Enslaved Africans in Portuguese Trash Dump," *Forbes*, March 22, 2019.

12   ***"atlantic is a sea of bones":*** Lucille Clifton, *The Collected Poems of Lucille Clifton 1965–2010*, ed. Kevin Young and Michael S. Glaser (Rochester, NY: BOA Editions Limited, 2015), 268.

14   ***white Europeans came to this country:*** C. L. Franklin, *Give Me This Mountain: Life History and Selected Sermons*, ed. Jeff Todd Titon (Champaign: University of Illinois Press, 1989), 81.

23   ***When the white man came to Africa:*** James Baldwin, *The Fire Next Time* (New York: Dial Press, 1963), 45.

24   ***handing down of the fire:*** Sam Lee and Joan Mills, "Tending the Flame," *Performance Research: A Journal of the Performing Arts* 24, no. 1 (2019): 104.

Chapter 2

36   ***"There is no music like that music":*** Baldwin, *The Fire Next Time*, 33.

Chapter 3

53   ***"look for the helpers":*** Fred Rogers and Barry Head, *Mister Rogers Talks With Parents* (Rochester, New York: Berkley Books, 1983), 183.

54   ***"Who can save a child":*** Henri Nouwen, *The Wounded Healer: Ministry in Contemporary Society* (New York: Doubleday, 1979), 72.

55 *"Jesus is God's wounded healer":* Nouwen, *The Wounded Healer*, 93.

58 *she "named things and/as she named":* Leslie Marmon Silko, *Ceremony* (New York: Viking Press, 1977), 1.

61 *"luminous darkness":* Howard Thurman, *The Luminous Darkness: A Personal Interpretation of the Anatomy of Segregation and the Ground of Hope* (New York: Harper and Row, 1965).

62 *"To know the dark, go dark":* Wendell Berry, "To Know the Dark," *Selected Poems of Wendell Berry* (Berkeley, CA: Counterpoint, 1999), 84.

Chapter 4

69 *"shit that weighs us down":* Toni Morrison, *Song of Solomon* (New York: Knopf, 1977), 179.

72 *"What, then, is the word":* Howard Thurman, *Jesus and the Disinherited* (Boston: Beacon Press, 1996), 1.

Chapter 5

81 *"The cross and the lynching tree":* James Cone, *The Cross and the Lynching Tree* (Maryknoll, NY: Orbis Books, 2011), 161.

82 *"They are attempting to perform impossibilities":* Charles Ball, *A Narrative of the Life and Adventures of Charles Ball, a Black Man, Who Lived Forty Years in Maryland, South Carolina and Georgia, as*

a Slave Under Various Masters, and Was One Year in the Navy with Commodore Barney, During the Late War (New York: Published by John S. Taylor, 1837).

87 ***"every atom of oxygen":*** "We Are Stardust," American Museum of Natural History, https://www.amnh.org/exhibitions/permanent/the-universe/stars/a-spectacular-stellar-finale/we-are-stardust.

93 ***"There are many forces":*** Howard Thurman, *Disciplines of the Spirit* (Richmond, IN: Friends United Press, 1963), 62.

94 ***"Whose standards am I following?":*** Elise M. Edwards, "'Do the Work Your Soul Must Have': In Remembrance of Rev. Dr. Katie Geneva Cannon," *Feminism and Religion,* August 19, 2018, https://feminismandreligion.com/2018/08/19/do-the-work-your-soul-must-have-in-remembrance-of-rev-dr-katie-geneva-cannon-by-elise-m-edwards/.

Chapter 6

103 ***"And you're STILL jim crowing me":*** Langston Hughes, *The Collected Poems of Langston Hughes* (New York: Vintage, 1985), 281.

105 ***One statistic concerning the GI Bill:*** Linda J. Bilmes and Cornell William Brooks, "The GI Bill Was One of the Worst Racial Injustices of the 20th Century. Congress Can Fix It," *Boston Globe,* February 23, 2022.

Chapter 7

119 ***"Did you hear about the rose":*** Tupac Shakur, *The Rose That Grew from Concrete* (New York: Pocket Books, 1999), 22.

122 ***Women of childbearing age:*** "Incarceration of Women Is Growing Twice as Fast as That of Men," Equal Justice Initiative, May 11, 2018, https://eji.org/news/female-incarceration-growing-twice-as-fast-as-male-incarceration/.

124 ***"white collar crimes":*** Brian K. Payne, *White Collar Crimes: The Essentials* (Thousand Oaks, CA: Sage Publications, 2016).

Chapter 8

140 ***"past exonerative tense":*** Devorah Blachor, "How to Use the Past Exonerative Tense to Uphold White Supremacy," *McSweeney's*, published June 1, 2020, https://www.mcsweeneys.net/articles/how-to-use-the-past-exonerative-tense-to-uphold-white-supremacy.

141 ***"one of the officer's rounds":*** Jonathan Moreno-Medina, Aurélie Ouss, Patrick Bayer, and Bocar Ba, "Officer-Involved: The Media Language of Police Killings," Sciences Po LIEPP Working Paper, 2023, https://sciencespo.hal.science/hal-04110697/document.

142 ***"Cheap grace is the grace":*** Dietrich Bonhoeffer, *The Cost of Discipleship* (New York: Macmillan, 1966), 44.

143 ***"unconditional love is the most powerful":*** Bernie Siegel, *Love, Medicine and Miracles: Lessons Learned about Self-Healing from a*

Surgeon's Experience with Exceptional Patients (New York: Harper Collins, 2011).

Chapter 9

153 ***Medical school students are still:*** Harriet A. Washington, *Medical Apartheid: The Dark History of Medical Experimentation on Black Americans from Colonial Times to the Present* (New York: Vintage, 2008).

Chapter 10

174 ***stress "literally wears down your heart":*** Arline Geronimus, quoted in "How Poverty and Racism 'Weather' the Body, Accelerating Aging and Disease," National Public Radio, March 28, 2023, https://www.npr.org/sections/health-shots/2023/03/28/1166404485/weathering-arline-geronimus-poverty-racism-stress-health.

Chapter 11

184 ***"We conspire to not remember":*** M. Shawn Copeland, "Memory, #BlackLivesMatter, and Theologians," *Political Theology*, volume 17.1, March 2016, politicaltheology.com.